Overcomer's Handbook

A Practical Guide to Victory in Christ

M.L. Fear

Marie L. Bergstrom Memorial Edition

To identify Overcomers in Christ resources, look for the Overcomer's Cross. This meaningful emblem combines an " α " for all life controlling problems with a cross for victory in Christ.

This registered trademark may not be duplicated without written permission from Overcomers in Christ.

Overcomer's Handbook, A practical guide to victory in Christ
ISBN 0-9670856-0-8
Seventh printing 1999
Copyright © 1986, 1989, 1991, 1993, 1998, 2000 M. L. Fear
Published by Overcomers in Christ
Cover by Todd Eby
All rights reserved. Written permission must be secured from the author to reproduce any part of this book, except for brief quotations in critical reviews or articles.

Unless otherwise noted, the Bible version used in this publication is the New International Version, Copyright © 1973, 1978, 1984, International Bible Society. Used by permission of Zondervan Bible Publishers. (Scripture quotations in bold type with occasional clarifying words in brackets.)

Section Four adapted from: Steps to Freedom in Christ © 1996 Neil T. Anderson, Regal Books, Ventura, CA 93003. Used with permission.

This Handbook belongs to:

Name: _____

Date: _____

> *You now hold in your hands a complete guide to victory in Christ! The simple format is ideal for personal devotions, one-on-one mentoring, and support groups. Sunday School and Bible study teachers, see pages 43-44 for an alternative format.*

CONTENTS

SECTION ONE— *THE WARM UP (Introduction)*

Welcome 8

What Is Christ-Centered Recovery? 9

Who Needs Recovery? 10

Where Are You? 12

How To Change 13

SECTION TWO— *THE STARTING LINE*

(How To Become God's Child) 15

SECTION THREE— *GET READY (Setting The Pace)*

Getting Focused 42

Coaches' Corner 43

SECTION FOUR— *GET SET (Steps To Freedom In Christ)*

Preparation 46

My History 48

Step One: Counterfeit vs. Real 51

Step Two: Deception vs. Truth 59

Step Three: Bitterness vs. Forgiveness 69

Step Four: Rebellion vs. Submission 75

Step Five: Pride vs. Humility 79

Step Six: Bondage vs. Freedom 83

Step Seven: Curses vs. Blessings 89

Aftercare 92

Who I Am In Christ 95

SECTION FIVE— *GO FOR THE GOALS (Workbook/Leader's Guide)*

Using Go For The Goals 98

Goal One: Truth 99

Goal Two: Attitude 107

Goal Three: Health 115

Goal Four: Decisions 123

Goal Five: Faith 131

The *Overcomer's Handbook* offers a compassionate blend of God 's grace and truth that touches hearts and changes lives.

Goal Six: Forgiveness 139

Goal Seven: Surrender 147

Goal Eight: Devotions 155

Goal Nine: Fellowship (Includes Amends Action Sheet) 163

Goal Ten: Inventory 173

Goal Eleven: Victory 183

Goal Twelve: Outreach 191

The Overcomer's Covenant In Christ 199

SECTION SIX—MARATHON ESSENTIALS (Important Help)

Meanings That Matter (Definitions) 202

Understanding The Bible 204

Power Through Prayer 205

Choosing A Church Family (Includes Statement of Faith) 206

Seeking Additional Help 208

Avoiding Relapse 209

Recommended Resources 210

SECTION SEVEN—FELLOW RUNNERS (Testimonies)

We're Family 214

The Overcomers in Christ Story 215

Member Interviews

Beverly V. 217

Bob W. 219

DeDee C. 221

Dennis F. 223

Ed B. 225

Glen C. 227

Jill B. 229

Julia P. 231

Lori W. 233

Mike H. 235

Pat B. 237

Tammy J. 239

"Valorie" 241

This section contains testimonies from people who have overcome addiction and dysfunction. However, the Overcomer's Handbook *can help ANYONE improve their relationship with God and others.*

Contents continued...

SECTION EIGHT— *TEAMS IN TRAINING* (Support Group Know-How)

Support Group Guidelines 244

Support Group Overview 246

Servant-Leaders 249

Getting Started 253

Meeting How To 255

Frequently Asked Questions 262

Institutional Groups Only 266

The Overcomer's Prayer 272

Way To Go (suggested format) .... inside back cover

The Christian life is a team effort.

Thank you to the many friends who helped make this book possible.

To God be the glory!

Section One

THE WARM UP
Introduction

Those who hope in the Lord will soar like eagles. Isaiah 40:31

- Welcome
- What Is Christ-Centered Recovery?
- Who Needs Recovery?
- Where Are You?
- How To Change

Welcome

Welcome to Overcomers in Christ. We gladly share with you the comfort and hope we have found in Jesus Christ. His unconditional love and victory at the cross give us the strength to overcome.

We freely admit that we cannot overcome our problems by ourselves. Life's difficulties and our shortcomings make us aware of our deep need for Jesus Christ. **"Surely He has borne our griefs and carried our sorrows."** In Christ, we do not see ourselves as victims but victors! No difficulty is too big or too small for Him.

Confidentiality Reminder: What is said in support group, stays there.

Nothing less than a personal, ongoing relationship with Jesus Christ brings lasting peace and satisfaction. In Him, we have found a fulfilling life that brings glory to God and joy to others. Jesus said, **"Come to Me, all you who are weary and burdened, and I will give you rest."**

We do not tell each other what to do or take responsibility for anyone else's recovery. Instead, we apply God's Word and the *Overcomer's Handbook* to our own lives. **"[God's] Word is a lamp to my feet and a light for my path."**

We offer you our friendship and a safe place to share your feelings and burdens. If you do not know Jesus, we understand. We didn't always know Him either. Please let us introduce you to our dearest Friend. You can find the new life and fellowship we have found in our Lord Jesus Christ.

Scripture references: Isaiah 53:4; Matthew 11:28; Psalms 119:105

The road to recovery leads to the cross.

WHAT IS CHRIST-CENTERED RECOVERY?

Christ-centered recovery is not so much *from something* as *to Someone*. "**You turned *to God from idols* to serve the living and true God**." The idols in our lives are revealed by the motive behind how we spend our time and money. True recovery comes as we find our identity, acceptance, and purpose in the Lord Jesus Christ.

Who needs recovery? Anyone whose relationship with God, family, and others falls short of God's standard. In other words, we all do to some degree. Some people like to think of recovery as spiritual growth. That's exactly right because recovery means allowing Christ to control every area of our lives.

> True recovery means finding our identity, acceptance, and purpose in the Lord Jesus Christ.

Christ's victory over sin on the cross provides the foundation for recovery. Sinful behavior is simply an attempt to meet our needs elsewhere than in Christ. We overcome life controlling habits to the extent that we find our deepest needs met in Him.

Recovery begins when we become God's child, but it does not end there. Genuine recovery is only possible as we allow Christ on the throne of our lives. Surrendering to the Lord gives Him His rightful place at the center of all that we think and do. Anything less holds us back from the purpose for which God created us. (Scripture reference: 1 Thess. 1:9b)

The Great Overcomer Cares

It is our prayer that this *Overcomer's Handbook* will help you experience the tender love and healing power of Jesus Christ. No matter how big or small the problems you face, He will help you find victory. Christ is the solution to all life's problems including sin, sorrow, and death. (He not only *has* the answer, but He *is* the answer.)

> Dear Jesus, I have a problem... it's me.
>
> Dear child, I have the answer... it's Me.

And who is Jesus Christ? He is the eternal Son of God who always was and always will be. He is our Creator and the Lord of the universe. Jesus had no sin of His own, but He came into the world to save sinners like you and me. By dying on the cross for our sins, Christ totally defeated Satan. He rose again from the dead as the great Overcomer. He lives so that we too can become overcomers rather than live in defeat.

You are holding Christ-centered recovery know-how in your hands right now. The key to benefiting from this Bible-based material is to let it change how you think. Therefore, do not attempt to work through the Handbook at a rapid pace. Instead, proceed at a rate which will allow you to absorb its life-changing truth into your life.

What Is Christ-Centered Recovery?

WHO NEEDS RECOVERY?

Personal Evaluation

If you do *not* feel that you have any questionable habits, substitute the brief inventory on page 181. Otherwise, use the evaluation below for each habit or relationship in question. Simply check the statements which are true. The more check marks, the greater your need for recovery.

Spiritual Checkup

_____ 1. This habit or relationship disturbs my inner peace.

_____ 2. This habit or relationship makes me feel distant from God.

_____ 3. This habit or person robs me of time alone with God.

_____ 4. This habit or person causes me to avoid fellowship with Christian people.

_____ 5. This habit or person causes me to compromise my values.

_____ 6. I am ashamed of this habit or relationship and sometimes lie about it.

_____ 7. This habit or relationship takes time or money that should be given to God and/or my family.

_____ 8. Sometimes I feel so trapped by this habit or person that I think about taking my life.

> Depending on Christ means using the resources He makes available. It does *not* mean refusing to take action.

Physical Checkup

_____ 1. This habit or relationship damages my health.

_____ 2. My energy level is lower because of involving myself in this habit or relationship.

_____ 3. If I attempt to stop this habit or relationship, I experience withdrawal symptoms.

_____ 4. This habit or relationship disturbs my normal sleeping habits.

_____ 5. As a result of this habit or relationship, I do not eat properly.

_____ 6. This habit or relationship has caused me to go to the doctor for help.

_____ 7. I use this habit or person to feel good or to get high.

_____ 8. Relatives of mine have had problems with addiction.

Mental Checkup

_____ 1. This habit or person leaves me confused and unable to think clearly.

_____ 2. This habit or person causes me to do things that make no sense.

_____ 3. This habit or relationship makes me feel that my life is out of control.

_____ 4. This habit or relationship affects my ability to follow through on things I need to do.

_____ 5. Thinking about this habit or relationship leaves me mentally exhausted.

_____ 6. I have thought about seeing a mental health professional about this habit or relationship.

_____ 7. This habit or person occupies my thoughts much of the time.

_____ 8. I feel the need to break this habit or relationship but have been unable to do so.

Emotional Checkup

> **Any relationship not based on faithfulness to Christ will end in disappointment or worse.**

_____ 1. This habit or relationship causes me to feel lonely and isolated.

_____ 2. I involve myself in this habit or relationship as an escape.

_____ 3. I use this habit or relationship as a way to handle stress.

_____ 4. When someone suggests that I need help to control this habit or limit this relationship, I get angry.

_____ 5. This habit or person causes me to do things I later regret.

_____ 6. I use this habit or person to increase my self-confidence.

_____ 7. I become uncomfortable if this habit or person becomes unavailable.

_____ 8. It takes more of this habit or person to get the feeling I want than it once did.

Social Checkup

_____ 1. My social circle has gotten smaller since involving myself with this habit or person.

_____ 2. This habit or person causes me to become irresponsible.

_____ 3. Because of this habit or person, I feel like a misfit.

_____ 4. This habit or person causes me to be inconsiderate of others.

_____ 5. This habit or relationship leaves me uncertain about what is normal.

_____ 6. This habit or person has caused arguments and broken friendships with people that I respect and love.

_____ 7. My fear of rejection determines what I say and do.

_____ 8. This habit or person makes it difficult to get along with others.

Who Needs Recovery? **11**

WHERE ARE YOU?

It takes time to move from denial to unconditional surrender, so be patient with yourself and others. Keep in mind that becoming God's child is the foundation upon which recovery rests.

When we step out of denial, we step into God's grace.

❑ DENIAL AND DEFENSIVENESS

"I don't have problems, so leave me alone." (This person often gets angry when encouraged toward recovery. When a person doesn't seem to care, it may be that he or she has given up hope.)

❑ HALFHEARTED ADMITTANCE

"My problems aren't that bad, and they're not my fault. Anyway, I can handle them on my own." (This person makes excuses, blames others, and refuses help.)

❑ HALFHEARTED INVOLVEMENT

"Maybe I do have problems—what can you do to fix them?" (This person expects others to solve his problems instead of working a Christ-centered recovery plan.)

❑ TOTAL ACCEPTANCE

"I accept the responsibility to seek recovery in Christ." (This person faces his problems, realizing that recovery demands personal involvement with a Christ-centered support system that provides guidance and accountability.)

God wants the very best for us, and the very best is Himself.

❑ UNCONDITIONAL SURRENDER

"I surrender myself to Jesus Christ as Lord." (This person makes a commitment to allow the Lord Jesus to control every area of his life. The *Overcomer's Handbook* can help develop this deeper relationship with Jesus Christ.)

12   *Where Are You?*

HOW TO CHANGE

Only the Lord Jesus can give you new life and bring about lasting change. You might as well try to build a house on quicksand as to seek new life apart from Christ. (If you don't know for sure that you have a relationship with God, the Starting Line on pages 15-40 is especially for you.)

If nothing changes, nothing changes.

I *CAN* LET JESUS CHANGE MY LIFE.

Listen to and believe what God says in His Word.
Identify and work with a godly sponsor-mentor.*
Fellowship with a Christ-centered support group.
Establish the habit of continual prayer and praise.

I *CAN* PROGRESS TOWARD THE GOALS.

Get into my Bible and Handbook regularly.
Open my mind to think deeply about God's truth.
Apply and act on what I learn.
Lean on the Lord instead of my own strength.
Spend time with godly people as often as possible.

I *CAN* PARTICIPATE IN A SUPPORT GROUP.

Go to group regularly and on time.
Remember to encourage others.
Open up rather than pretend I've got no problems.
Use the phone or mail to keep in touch.
Pray regularly for other members' needs.

I *CAN* BENEFIT BY BEING SPONSORED.

Stay in contact with my sponsor-mentor.*
Pray with him or her regularly.
Openly share my feelings.
Never hesitate to ask questions.
Shoulder my own responsibility.
Open myself to his or her suggestions.
Realize my sponsor cannot "fix" me.
Expect him or her to hold me accountable.
Discover the joy of fellowship.

God's truth will set you free only as you believe and obey Him.

*See the definition on page 203.

Notes

The reason
self-help groups
don't help is
that self got
self in trouble in
the first place!

Section Two

THE STARTING LINE
How To Become God's Child

Those who hope in the Lord will soar like eagles. Isaiah 40:31

This section tells in simple words how to become God's child and is illustrated by children. Jesus said, *"I praise you, Father, Lord of heaven and earth, because you have hidden these things from the wise and learned and revealed them to little children." "I tell you the truth, unless you become like little children, you will never enter the kingdom of heaven."* Matthew 11:25; 18:3

How can I be sure that the Bible is God's word?

I know that the Bible is God's word because:

A. Fulfilled prophecy proves it! Not a single Bible prediction has ever been proved wrong. Things foretold thousands of years before have come true to the smallest detail. This could not possibly happen by mere chance. Only God can predict the future with total accuracy. **"I tell you the truth, until heaven and earth disappear, not the smallest letter, not the least stroke of a pen, will by any means disappear from [God's word] until everything is accomplished."** Matthew 5:18

B. All 66 books in the Bible fit together perfectly. The more than 40 writers had to deal with difficult topics and stake their lives on what they wrote! Yet they all expressed the same viewpoint about God and mankind. God obviously told them what to say. **"Above all, you must understand that no Scripture came about by the prophet's own interpretation. For prophecy never had its origin in the will of man, but men spoke from God as they were carried along by the Holy Spirit."** 2 Peter 1:20-21

C. The Bible changes lives like no other book. Anyone who reads the Bible, and puts it into practice, will be completely transformed. It is the only book that people can read every day for a lifetime and always find something to meet their need. No wonder the Bible is the most widely read and best loved book in history! **"All Scripture is God-breathed and is useful for teaching, rebuking, correcting and training in righteousness."** 2 Timothy 3:16

Make It Personal

What proves to me that the Bible is God's Word? (Be sure to allow the Scriptures on the facing page to influence your answer.)

_____
_____
_____
_____
_____
_____
_____
_____
_____
_____
_____
_____

The Bible is the only book written by an Author who cannot lie and who never changes.

THE STARTING LINE
How To Become God's Child

Notes

The Starting Line 17

Why is it so important to become God's child?

The Bible tells me:

A. To fulfill the purpose for which God made me, I must become His child. Only as God's child can I find lasting fulfillment and meaning. **"I have come that they may have life, and have it to the full."** John 10:10

B. By becoming God's child, I can overcome fear and have a relationship with Him as my heavenly Father. **"You did not receive a spirit that makes you a slave again to fear, but you received the Spirit of sonship."** Romans 8:15

C. I will live forever in heaven or hell, depending on whether I become God's child. Hell is an awful place, and God does not want me to go there. He has prepared a wonderful home for me in heaven. But to go there, I must be born into God's family. **"Jesus declared, 'I tell you the truth, no one can see the kingdom of God unless he is born again.'"** John 3:3

Make It Personal

For what reasons is it essential for me to become God's child? (Be sure to allow the Scriptures on the facing page to influence your answer.)

_____

_____

_____

_____

_____

_____

_____

_____

_____

_____

_____

Only God's children can enter heaven.

Notes

The Starting Line 19

Isn't everyone God's child?

The Bible tells me:

A. When I was born physically, I got human life. But when I am born spiritually, I get everlasting life and become part of God's family. **"Flesh gives birth to flesh, but the Spirit gives birth to spirit. You should not be surprised at my saying, 'You must be born again.'"** John 3:6-7

B. Everyone has been born in sin and needs a spiritual birthday to become God's child. This new birth comes about by accepting God's gift of eternal life. **"Jesus declared, 'I tell you the truth, no one can see the kingdom of God unless he is born again.'" "For all have sinned and fall short of the glory of God."** John 3:3; Romans 3:23

C. Saying a prayer or doing good works does not make anyone God's child. If I had to do something to earn God's gift, then it wouldn't be a gift. **"For it is by grace you have been saved, through faith—and this is not from yourselves, it is the gift of God—not by works, so that no one can boast."** Ephesian 2:8-9

Make It Personal

How, when and where have I been born again or do I still need to be? (Be sure to allow the Scriptures on the facing page to influence your answer.)

_____
_____
_____
_____
_____
_____
_____
_____
_____
_____
_____
_____

Going to church does not make me God's child any more than going to the zoo makes me a monkey!

Notes

THE STARTING LINE
How To Become God's Child

The Starting Line 21

How will becoming God's child change my life?

The Bible tells me:

A. I will have a loving Father in heaven to take care of me and a home with Him forever. No matter what I have done, my sins will all be forgiven. **"In [Christ] we have redemption through his blood, the forgiveness of sins, according to the riches of God's grace that he lavished on us."** Ephesians 1:7-8

B. Nothing or no one can separate me from God's unconditional love and acceptance. **"Neither death nor life, neither angels nor demons, neither the present nor the future, nor any powers, neither height nor depth, nor anything else in all creation, will be able to separate us from the love of God that is in Christ Jesus our Lord."** Romans *8:38-39*

C. My heart will be filled with God's peace and joy. **"Peace I leave with you; my peace I give you. I do not give to you as the world gives. Do not let your heart be troubled and do not be afraid."** John 14:27

The Starting Line

Make it Personal

What difference will becoming God's child make in my life? (Be sure to allow the Scriptures on the facing page to influence your answer.)

When I become God's child, I become royalty!

Notes

The Starting Line 23

With all the people in the world, how do I know God cares about me?

The Bible tells me:

A. Jesus knows me and loves me as though I were the only person in the world. He knows me so well, He numbers the hairs on my head! **"Are not five sparrows sold for two pennies? Yet not one of them is forgotten by God. Indeed, the very hairs of your head are all numbered. Don't be afraid; you are worth more than many sparrows."** Luke 12:6-7

B. God formed me and knew me even before I was born. **"For you created my inmost being; you knit me together in my mother's womb. I praise you for I am fearfully and wonderfully made; your works are wonderful, I know that full well. My frame was not hidden from you when I was made in the secret place. When I was woven together in the depths of the earth, your eyes saw my unformed body. All the days [appointed] for me were written in your book before one of them came to be."** Psalm 139:13-16

C. God proved His love by giving His only Son to die for me. **"God demonstrates his own love for us in this: While we were still sinners, Christ died for us."** Romans 5:8

The Starting Line

Make It Personal

How do I know God cares about me? (Be sure to allow the Scriptures on the facing page to influence your answer.)

_____

_____

_____

_____

_____

_____

_____

_____

_____

_____

_____

When I realize that God gave His only Son to die for me, how can I doubt His love?

Notes

The Starting Line 25

Why does God let bad things happen?

The Bible tells me:

A. Sin brought suffering and death into the world, and that brings pain to us all. **"Sin entered the world through one man, and death through sin, and in this way death came to all men because all sinned."** Romans 5:12

B. Jesus won the victory over sin and death. He promises to bring good out of all my difficulties if I love and trust Him. **"We know that in all things God works for the good of those who love Him…" Thanks be to God! He gives us the victory through our Lord Jesus Christ."** Romans 8:28; 1 Corinthians 15:56-57

C. Jesus paid for my ticket to heaven with His own blood. He wants me to spend forever with Him where there is no sin, no pain, and no death. **"Do not let your hearts be troubled. Trust in God; trust also in me. In my Father's house are many rooms; if it were not so, I would have told you. I am going there to prepare a place for you. And if I go and prepare a place for you, I will come back and take you to be with me that you also may be where I am."** John 14:1-3

The Starting Line

> ## Make It Personal
>
> How can I find victory over the suffering that sin has caused? (Be sure to allow the Scriptures on the facing page to influence your answer.)
>
> _____
> _____
> _____
> _____
> _____
> _____
> _____
> _____
> _____
> _____
> _____
> _____
> _____

Satan laughs when God gets blamed for sin and suffering.

Notes

What if I don't feel worthy to be God's child?

The Bible tells me:

A. It's God's mercy (not how deserving I am) that makes a way for me to be brought into God's family. To try to add to what Jesus has already done on the cross would be like trying to improve something that is already perfect. **"He saved us, not because of righteous things we had done, but because of His mercy."** Titus 3:4-5

B. Even if I was so good I only sinned once a day, I'd still have 365 sins every year! God cannot let even one sin into heaven, so He sent Jesus to die for all my sins. **"Here is a trustworthy saying that deserves full acceptance: Christ Jesus came into the world to save sinners."** 1 Timothy 1:15

C. The price God paid for me determines my worth. Jesus shed His precious blood to make me His child. **"But now in Christ Jesus, you who once were far away have been brought near through the blood of Christ."** Ephesians 2:13

Make It Personal

What has God done to demonstrate how much He values me? (Be sure to allow the Scriptures on the facing page to influence your answer.)

_____
_____
_____
_____
_____
_____
_____
_____
_____
_____
_____
_____

The price God paid for me determines my worth.

Notes

The Starting Line 29

What does the cross mean to me?

The Bible tells me:

A. Jesus died on the cross in my place and finished all the work to pay for my sins. **"Christ died for sins once for all, the righteous for the unrighteous to bring you to God."** 1 Peter 3:18

B. Jesus' empty tomb proves that God accepted His payment for my sins. **"For what I received I passed on to you as of first importance: that Christ died for our sins according to the Scriptures, and that he was buried, that he was raised on the third day..."** 1 Corinthians 15:3-4

C. God gives eternal life to me the moment I accept Jesus as my sin-bearer and Lord. **"To all who received Him, to those who believed in His name, He gave the right to become the children of God."** John 1:12

Make It Personal

Why did Jesus die on the cross? (Be sure to allow the Scriptures on the facing page to influence your answer.)

_____
_____
_____
_____
_____
_____
_____
_____
_____
_____
_____
_____

You get God's gift the same way you get any gift— you accept it.

Notes

How can I get eternal life and become God's child?

The Bible tells me:

"God so loved the world that he gave his one and only Son that whoever believes in him shall not perish but have eternal life." John 3:16

By taking John 3:16 phrase by phrase, I can better understand what God is saying to me.

A. **"For God so loved the world** (Since I'm in the world, God loves me too.)

B. **"that He gave His one and only Son** (God gave Jesus to die for my sins on the cross.)

C. **"that whoever** (Whoever includes me.)

D. **"believes in Him** (To believe means to take God at His word that He means what He says.)

E. **"shall not perish** (I'll never go to that awful place called Hell.)

F. **"but have eternal life."** ("Have" means eternal life can be mine right now simply by taking God at His word.)

The Starting Line

Make It Personal

What is God saying to me in John 3:16? (Please carefully ponder the facing page before you answer.)

_____

_____

_____

_____

_____

_____

_____

_____

_____

_____

Don't focus on your feelings but on what God's word is saying to you.

Notes

The Starting Line   33

Am I making a simple thing difficult?

The Bible tells me:

A. God made the way to heaven simple enough for a child to understand. I need to come to Him in child-like faith. Jesus said, **"I tell you the truth, unless you become like little children, you will never enter the kingdom of heaven." "I praise you, Father, Lord of heaven and earth, because you have hidden these things from the wise and learned and revealed them to little children."** Matthew 18:3; 11:25

B. God's word was written so I can know without a doubt that I have eternal life. **"I write these things to you who believe in the name of the Son of God so that you may know that you have eternal life."** 1 John 5:13

C. I can depend on God to keep His word because He cannot lie. **"It is impossible for God to lie, [so] we who have fled to take hold of the hope offered to us may be greatly encouraged."** Hebrews 6:18

The Starting Line

Make It Personal

Am I coming to God in faith or am I trying to analyze Him? (Be sure to allow the Scriptures on the facing page to influence your answer.)

_____
_____
_____
_____
_____
_____
_____
_____
_____
_____
_____

It's not *how much* faith I have, but *Who* my faith is in that counts.

Notes

The Starting Line   35

God says it,
I believe it, and
that settles it!

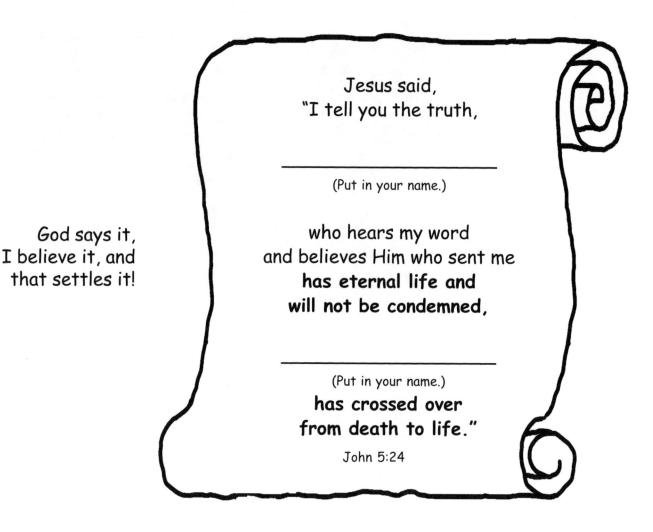

Jesus said,
"I tell you the truth,

_____
(Put in your name.)

who hears my word
and believes Him who sent me
**has eternal life and
will not be condemned,**

_____
(Put in your name.)
**has crossed over
from death to life."**

John 5:24

Make It Personal

What is God saying to me in the verse above?

_____
_____
_____
_____
_____
_____
_____
_____
_____
_____

How can I tell God thank you for what He has done for me?

Most of all, God wants His children to live to please Him. But He also wants us to tell Him thank you. In your own words, write a thank you prayer below. Then talk to Jesus by praying your prayer aloud.

Date: _____

Dear Lord Jesus,

_____
_____
_____
_____
_____
_____
_____
_____
_____

Signed: _____

The Starting Line

What does it mean to be part of God's family?

The Bible tells me:

A. I am secure forever in God's hand. **"I give them eternal life, and they shall never perish; no one can snatch them out of my hand. My Father, who has given them to me, is greater than all, no one can snatch them out of my Father's hand."** John 10:28-29

B. Being born into God's family is the beginning of a whole new life. **"If anyone is in Christ, he is a new creation; the old has gone, the new has come!" "I have been crucified with Christ and I no longer live, but Christ lives in me. The life I live in the body, I live by faith in the Son of God, who loved me and gave himself for me."** 2 Corinthians 5:17; Galatians 2:20

C. God's Word is my necessary daily food. It is a love-letter from my heavenly Father and my life instruction manual. I grow by feeding on God's Word and by applying it to my daily life. **"Like newborn babies, crave pure spiritual milk, so that by it you may grow up in your salvation."** 1 Peter 2:2

Make It Personal

How can I grow in my new life? (Be sure to allow paragraph C on the facing page to influence your answer.)

_____

_____

_____

_____

_____

_____

_____

_____

_____

_____

_____

What if I'm still unclear about whether I have eternal life?

If you don't know for sure that you have eternal life, please repeat Section Two, or ask a born again person to help you.

I can look at what God's Word says for myself. Here's how I can easily find any Bible verse:

book	chapter	colon	verse
John	3	:	16

The Bible table of contents gives the book's page number.
The number *before* the colon identifies which chapter.
The number *after* the colon identifies which verse.

The Starting Line 39

Notes

Life is not a sprint, it's a marathon. It takes the power of Christ to go the distance.

Section Three

GET READY
Setting The Pace

Those who hope in the Lord will soar like eagles. Isaiah 40:31

- Getting Focused
- Coaches' Corner

GETTING FOCUSED

Whether you've known the Lord for years, or are searching for Him, the *Overcomer's Handbook* will meet you where you are. This life-changing resource will help you improve your relationships with God and the people around you. As a result, you'll come to experience victory on a daily basis.

Don't let the simplicity of this Handbook fool you. It effectively and thoroughly deals with the issues that cause pain and lack of progress. As a participant in Overcomers in Christ, you will focus on four vital areas:

Rebirth
You can experience spiritual rebirth as you visit the cross at the "Starting Line" (Section Two). If you've already been born again, you will sharpen your skills for leading others to Christ.

Release

To develop a personal relationship with God means to learn to love what He loves and hate what He hates.

Most of us have bondages of one sort or another as evidenced by life controlling problems. Section Four "Get Set" (pages 45-96) walks us through an encounter with God to overcome our obstacles. This section is best done before advancing to "Go for the Goals" but may be done at any time you are ready.

Reprogramming
A video replay of our thoughts would quickly indicate that most of us need to reprogram our minds. Section Five (pages 97-200) helps us reject lies and misbeliefs and embrace the truth. We learn to allow Christ to control our thoughts as the key to victory in Christ. Sections Six and Seven inform, motivate, and support us along the way.

Reproduction
Abundant life in Christ is too good to keep to ourselves! Goal Twelve (page 191) and Section Eight (pages 243-272) help us help others live in victory.

Jesus' messages were approximately 30% information and 70% application. His parables give stories about life to explain small nuggets of truth. Likewise, the *Overcomer's Handbook* focuses on personal application of truth to our everyday lives.

This Handbook is ideally formatted for personal devotions, one-on-one mentoring, and support groups. For personal devotions and mentoring, simply proceed prayerfully through the material as it is laid out. Support group leaders can benefit from the practical guidance in "Teams In Training" on pages 243-272. Bible study/and or Sunday School teachers can follow the format on the facing page. May the Lord go with you as you journey onward.

42   *Getting Focused*

COACHES' CORNER

(For Bible Study and/or Sunday School Class teachers ONLY. Support group leaders, refer to "Teams In Training" pages 243-272.)

This adapted format suits a thirteen week Sunday School class or Bible study of 60 to 90 minutes. Open and close each class with prayer for God's help and victory. Pray regularly that the Holy Spirit will work in your students' lives and allow Him to do the same in yours.

The *Overcomer's Handbook* offers a life-plan rather than a course from which to graduate. However, this thirteen week course will give your students a foundation for Christ-centered recovery and whet their appetite for more. Make yourself available after class for those who have further questions. Also, inform your students about Overcomers in Christ support groups and other Christ-centered resources.

Example is not the best way to teach, it's the only way.

You will spend most of your time in "Go for the Goals" (Section Five, pages 97-200). However, familiarize yourself with the other sections of the Handbook so you can utilize the resources and point them out to the class.

To begin:
Ask the class, "What is Christ-centered recovery?" Read and briefly discuss the material by that name on page 9. *Underscore the thought that recovery is another name for spiritual growth.* Have the class do the attitude and behavior inventory on page 181. Then ask them if they see any areas where they need recovery. They should all respond, "Yes." Now turn to page 12 and walk them through the five attitudes they might have.

Next go to "The Starting Line" (Section Two, page 15). Proceed through the entire section reading the questions and having students read the answers one alphabetical paragraph at a time. Spend extra time on the explanation of John 3:16 (page 32). Then ask the students to put their name in John 5:24 (page 36) and read it aloud. Help them understand that salvation does *not* depend on saying a prayer but on accepting the finished work of Christ.

Finally, give the class time to write their own thank you prayer to the Lord Jesus for paying their sin debt (page 37). Be aware that people will accept Christ as their Savior at any point in this section if you proceed slowly and prayerfully. Complete this entire section through page 39. (Don't be surprised if some *professing* Christians get genuinely born again as they go to the cross by faith.)

Those who know for sure they are God's children are ready to continue the study. Remember to recommend the Steps to Freedom (Section Four, pages 45-96) for people who feel unable to grow in their Christian walk. Otherwise, they will get no further than the Starting Line.

Coaches' Corner **43**

Assignment for next week:

Ask students to read Goal One, pages 99-106. They will need to spend a minimum of 10-15 minutes each day for five days and complete the assignments for paragraphs A through E. Students should come to class prepared to share.

Each week, for the next twelve weeks, lead the class through another Goal by discussing it and applying the Scriptures. You may bring in other verses to support the theme of the Goal and to help the class better understand its application. Discuss the application questions as time permits. Draw the students out rather than attempt to do all the talking.

Assignment for each week to follow:

Assign the same responsibility as above for each succeeding Goal. Be sure to refer students who want additional help to Overcomers in Christ or other Christ-centered resources.

> The one who learns most from a class is often the teacher.

Notes

44   *Coaches' Corner*

Section Four

Get Set:
Steps To Freedom In Christ

By Neil T. Anderson, Rich Miller, Dave Park
*Used and adapted by permission
of Freedom in Christ Ministries
and Regal Books*

Those who hope in the Lord will soar like eagles. Isaiah 40:31

- Preparation
- My History
- Counterfeit vs. Real
- Deception vs. Truth
- Bitterness vs. Forgiveness
- Rebellion vs. Submission
- Pride vs. Humility
- Bondage vs. Freedom
- Curses vs. Blessings
- Aftercare
- Who I Am In Christ

PREPARATION

NOTE: The "Steps To Freedom In Christ" (pages 45-96) involve an encounter with God that is best done early in recovery. But if you prefer, skip to page 97, and come back to the Steps to Freedom later. God is ready whenever you are.

If you have received Christ as your Savior, He has already set you free through His victory over sin and death on the cross. The question is: Are you living victoriously in Christ's freedom or are you still living in slavery?

How can you tell if you are *living free in Christ?* Freedom in Christ is having the desire and power to know, love, worship and obey God. It is the joyful liberty of knowing God's truth and walking according to God's truth in the power of the Holy Spirit. It is not a perfect life, for that is impossible this side of heaven. But it is a *growing, "abundant life"* in Christ (Jn. 10:10).

What God begins, He will complete.

If you are not experiencing that kind of freedom, it may be because you have not stood firm in the faith or lived according to who you are *in Christ*. Somehow you have allowed a yoke of slavery to put you back in bondage. It is your responsibility, however, to do whatever is needed to walk in your freedom in Christ. If you are a Christian, your eternal life is not at stake; you are safe and secure in Christ. But your daily victory is at stake if you choose not to walk according to the truth.

No matter how tough things might be for you spiritually right now, we've got great news for you! You are not a helpless victim caught in a tug-of-war match between two nearly equal but opposite heavenly superpowers—God and Satan. Only God is all-powerful, always present and all-knowing. Satan was defeated by Christ, the Victor at the Cross, so don't believe the lie that your situation is hopeless or that you are helpless against his attacks.

Satan knows you have authority over him in Christ, but he doesn't want you to know it. He is a liar and the only way he can have power over you is if you believe his lies.

Do the thing you fear, and the death of fear is certain.

The battle is for your mind. You may experience nagging thoughts like, "This isn't going to work," or "God doesn't love me," etc. Don't believe the devil's lies. If you believe Satan's deceptions, you will really struggle with making it through the "Steps to Freedom in Christ."

If you are working through the steps by yourself, don't pay any attention to accusing or threatening thoughts. If you are working with a trusted friend, pastor or counselor (which we heartily encourage), then tell him/her any thoughts you are having that are in opposition to what you are trying to do.

46   *Preparation*

Remember, the only power Satan has over you is the power of the lie. Expose the lie by getting it out in the open; then choose the truth, and the power of that lie is broken. In that way you will be able to maintain control during this session.

You must cooperate with the person who is trying to help you by sharing what is going on inside your mind. Also, if you experience any physical discomfort (such as headache, nausea, tightness in the throat, etc.), don't be alarmed. Just tell the person you are with so that he/she can pray for you. Don't let the devil set the agenda during this time; let the Holy Spirit call the shots.

Don't let the devil set the agenda.

As believers in Christ, we can pray with authority to stop any interference by Satan. Here is a prayer and declaration to get you going. Read them (and all the prayers and declarations in **bold type**) aloud.

Opening Prayer

Dear Heavenly Father, we know that You are right here in this room with us and that You are present in our lives right now. You are the only all-knowing, all-powerful, and ever-present God. We are completely dependent upon You because without Jesus Christ, we can do nothing. We choose to stand in the truth of Your Word, and we refuse to believe the devil's lies. We thank You that the risen Lord Jesus has all authority in heaven and on earth. Father, thank You that because we are in Christ we share His authority in order to make disciples and set captives free. We ask You to protect our minds and bodies during this time. Please fill us with the Holy Spirit so that He can guide us into all truth. We choose to submit to His guidance alone during this time. Please reveal to our minds everything that You want us to deal with today. We ask for and trust in Your wisdom. We pray all this in faith, in the name of Jesus. Amen.

Declaration

The battle is for your mind.

In the name and authority of the Lord Jesus Christ, we command Satan and all evil spirits to release their hold on (name) in order that (name) can be free to know and choose to do the will of God. As children of God, raised up and seated with Christ in the heavenly places, we agree that every enemy of the Lord Jesus Christ be bound. We say to Satan and all his evil workers that you cannot inflict any pain or in any way prevent God's will from being done today in (name's) life.

Preparation 47

My History

Before going through the Steps to Freedom, review the events of your life to discern specific areas that might need to be addressed.

Family History

- ❑ Religious history of parents and grandparents
- ❑ Home life from childhood through high school
- ❑ History of physical or emotional illness in the family
- ❑ Adoption, foster care, guardians

Personal History

- ❑ Spiritual journey (salvation: when, how and assurance of)
- ❑ Eating habits (bulimia, bingeing and purging, anorexia, compulsive eating)
- ❑ Addictions (drugs, alcohol, gambling, sexual, etc.)
- ❑ Prescription medications (what for?)
- ❑ Sleeping patterns and nightmares
- ❑ Rape or any sexual, physical, emotional abuse
- ❑ Thought life (obsessive, blasphemous, condemning, distracting thoughts, poor concentration, fantasy)
- ❑ Mental interference in church, prayer, or Bible study
- ❑ Emotional life (anger, anxiety, depression, bitterness, fears)

> "Do not let your heart be troubled and do not be afraid."
> John 14:27

Now you are ready to start going through the "Steps to Freedom in Christ." There are seven steps to help you experience freedom from your past. You will address the areas in which Satan commonly takes advantage of believers and where strongholds are often built.

Remember that the Lord Jesus Christ has already purchased your freedom over sin and Satan on the cross. Experiencing that freedom will be the result of what you choose to believe, confess, renounce and forgive. No one can do that for you, not even God. The battle for your mind will only be won as you personally choose the truth.

During each step, it is very important that you submit to God inwardly while resisting the devil outwardly. Do this by praying each prayer and making each declaration *out loud*. The prayers and declarations are all in **bold type** to remind you to do that.

> **We need to see ourselves as overcomers in those areas of life which would defeat us.**
> Marie Schilling

You will be taking a very thorough inventory of your life in order to make a rock-solid commitment to the truth. If your problems stem from another source not covered in these steps, you may need to seek professional help. If you are open and honest during this time, you will greatly benefit by becoming right with God and close to Him again.

May the Lord greatly touch your life during this time. He alone can and will give you the grace to make it through. Lean on His strength and wisdom, not on your own. And it is crucial that you work through all seven steps during one session. Take short breaks as you need them, but don't allow yourself to become discouraged and give up.

Remember, the freedom that Christ purchased for all believers on the cross is meant for you!

Notes

> The "Steps to Freedom in Christ" do not set you free. Who sets you free is Christ, and what sets you free is your response to Him in repentance and faith.
>
> Neil T. Anderson

Notes

Counterfeit vs. Real

The First Step

COUNTERFEIT VS. REAL

The first step toward experiencing your freedom in Christ is to renounce (verbally reject) all past or present involvement with occult practices, cult teachings and rituals, as well as non-Christian religions.

You must renounce any activity or group which denies Jesus Christ or offers guidance through any source other than the absolute authority of the Bible. Any group that requires dark, secret initiations, ceremonies, promises or pacts should also be renounced. Begin this step by praying aloud:

Dear Heavenly Father, I ask You to bring to my mind anything and everything that I have done knowingly or unknowingly that involves occult, cult, or non-Christian teachings or practices. I want to experience Your freedom by renouncing these things right now. In Jesus' name, I pray. Amen.

> Freedom comes on God's terms, not ours. God's terms always involve genuine turning away from sin followed by obedience to His commands.

Even if you took part in something and thought it was just a game or a joke, you need to renounce it. Satan will try to take advantage of anything he can in our lives, so it is wise to be as thorough as possible. Even if you were just standing by and watching others do it, you need to renounce your passive involvement. You may not have even realized at the time that what was going on was evil. Still, go ahead and renounce it.

Note the "Non-Christian Spiritual Checklist" on the facing page. List those things that the Lord brings to your mind. (Neil Anderson identifies many of the more common non-Christian groups and practices in his books. Editor)

If something comes to your mind, and you're not sure what to do about it, trust that the Spirit of God is answering the prayer you just prayed. Go ahead and renounce whatever it is.

After the checklist, there are some additional questions to help you become aware of other things you may need to renounce. Below those questions is a short prayer of confession and renunciation. *Pray it out loud, filling in the blanks with the groups, teachings or practices that the Holy Spirit has prompted you to renounce during this time of personal evaluation.*

Non-Christian Spiritual Checklist

List all those that you have participated in.

❏   Non-Christian religions or cults:

_____
_____
_____
_____
_____
_____

❏   Occult or violent video or computer games:

_____
_____
_____
_____
_____
_____

❏   Movies, TV shows, music, books, magazines or comics that the Lord is bringing to your mind *(especially those that glorified Satan, caused fear or nightmares, were gruesomely violent or stimulated the flesh).* List them below.

_____
_____
_____
_____
_____

1. Have you ever seen, heard or felt a spiritual being in your room?

2. Do you have recurring nightmares? (Specifically renounce any accompanying fear.)

3. Do you now have, or have you ever had, an imaginary friend, spirit guide, or "angel" offering you guidance or companionship? (If it has a name, renounce it by name.)

Counterfeit vs. Real   53

4. Have you ever heard voices in your head or had repeating, nagging thoughts such as, "I'm dumb," "I'm ugly," "Nobody loves me," "I can't do anything right," etc. as if there were a conversation going on inside your head? Explain.

_____

_____

_____

_____

_____

_____

Even a little lie is dangerous; it deteriorates the conscience.
Pablo Casals

5. Have you ever seen or been contacted by beings you thought were aliens?

6. Have you ever made a secret vow or pact?

7. Have you ever been involved in a satanic ritual of any kind or attended a concert in which Satan was the focus?

8. Have you had other spiritual experiences that would be considered out of the ordinary? Explain.

_____

_____

_____

_____

_____

_____

_____

_____

Once you have completed your checklist, confess and renounce each item you were involved in by praying the following prayer *out loud*:

Lord, I confess that I have participated in _____ _____. I know that it was evil and offensive in Your sight. Thank You for Your forgiveness. I renounce any and all involvement with _____, and I cancel out any and all ground that the enemy gained in my life through this activity. In Jesus' name, Amen.

54   *Counterfeit vs. Real*

We were created to worship the true and living God. In fact, the Father seeks those who will worship Him in spirit and in truth (Jn. 4:23). As children of God, "We know also that the Son of God has come and given us understanding, so that we may know Him Who is true. And we are in Him Who is true — even in His Son, Jesus Christ. He is the true God and eternal life" (1 Jn. 5:20 *NIV*).

Who or what is most important to us becomes that which we worship. Our thoughts, love, devotion, trust, adoration and obedience are directed to this object above all others. This object of worship is truly our God or god.

The apostle John follows the above passage with a warning, "Little children, guard yourselves from idols" (1 Jn. 5:21 *NASB*). An idol is a false god, any object of worship other than the true God.

Though we may not bow down to statues, it is easy for people and things of this world to become more important to us than the Lord Himself. The following prayer expresses the commitment of a heart that chooses to "worship the Lord your God and serve Him only" (Matt. 4: 10).

Dear Lord God, I know how easy it is to allow other things and other people to become more important to me than You. I also know that this is terribly offensive to Your holy eyes as You have commanded that I "shall have no other gods before You" (Exod. 20:3)**.**

I confess to You that I have not loved You with all my heart and soul and mind (Matt. 22:37)**. As a result I have sinned against You, violating the first and greatest commandment. I repent of and turn away from this idolatry and now choose to return to You, Lord Jesus, as my first love once again** (Rev. 2:4, 5)**.**

Please reveal to my mind now any and all idols in my life. I want to renounce each of them, and in so doing, cancel out any and all ground Satan may have gained in my life through my idolatry. In the name of Jesus, the true God, Amen.

> Who or what is most important to us becomes that which we worship.

As the Holy Spirit brings to your mind the things or people that have become more important to you than the true God, Jesus Christ, use the prayer on the opposite page (in **bold print**) to renounce them. The checklist below may be a help to you in recognizing those areas. Notice that most (if not all) of the areas listed below are not evil in themselves; they become idols when they take over God's rightful place as Lord of our lives.

- ❑   Ambition
- ❑   Money / Possessions
- ❑   Financial Security
- ❑   Church Activities

Counterfeit vs. Real   55

> Truth leads to freedom only when it is obeyed.
> Elisabeth Elliott

- ❑ Sports or Physical Fitness
- ❑ Ministry
- ❑ Work
- ❑ Friends
- ❑ Boyfriend / Girlfriend
- ❑ Spouse
- ❑ Children
- ❑ Parents
- ❑ Food or Any Substance
- ❑ Computers / Games / Software
- ❑ Rock Stars / Media Celebrities / Athletes
- ❑ TV / Movies / Music / Other Media
- ❑ Fun / Pleasure
- ❑ Appearance / Image
- ❑ Busyness / Activity
- ❑ Power / Control
- ❑ Popularity / Opinion of Others
- ❑ Knowledge / Being Right
- ❑ Hobbies

In the name of the true and living God, Jesus Christ, I renounce my worship of the false god of (name the idol). **I choose to worship only You, Lord, and ask You, Father, to enable me to keep this area of** (name the idol) **in its proper place in my life. In Jesus name, Amen.**

> "He who is in you is greater than he who is in the world."
> 1 John 4:4b NKJV

If you have been involved in satanic rituals or heavy occult activity (or you suspect it because of blocked memories, severe and recurring nightmares or sexual bondage or dysfunction), you need to say out loud the "Special Renunciation for Satanic Ritual Involvement" on the following page.

Read across the page, renouncing the first item in the column under "Domain of Darkness" and then announcing the first truth in the column under "Kingdom of Light." Continue down the page in that manner.

56   *Counterfeit vs. Real*

Special Renunciations for Satanic Ritual Involvement

Domain of Darkness

1. I renounce ever signing my name over or in having my name signed over to Satan by someone else.

2. I renounce any ritual where I was wed to Satan.

3. I renounce any and all covenants, agreements or promises that I made to Satan.

4. I renounce all satanic assignments for my life including duties, marriage and children.

5. I renounce all spirit guides assigned to me.

6. I renounce ever giving of my blood in the service of Satan.

7. I renounce ever eating flesh or drinking blood in satanic worship.

8. I renounce all guardians and Satanist parents that were assigned to me.

9. I renounce any baptism whereby I am identified with Satan.

10. I renounce any sacrifice made on my behalf by which Satan may claim ownership of me.

Kingdom of Light

1. I announce that my name is now written in the Lamb's Book of Life.

2. I announce that I am the Bride of Christ.

3. I announce that I have made a new covenant with Jesus Christ alone.

4. I announce and commit myself to know and to do only the will of God, and I accept His guidance for my life.

5. I announce and accept only the leading of the Holy Spirit.

6. I trust only in the shed blood of my Lord Jesus Christ.

7. By faith, I eat only the body and drink only the blood of the Lord Jesus in Holy Communion.

8. I announce that God is my Heavenly Father and the Holy Spirit is my guardian by whom I am sealed.

9. I announce that I have been baptized into Christ Jesus and my identity is now in Him.

10. I announce that only the sacrifice of Christ has any claim on me. I belong to Him. I have been purchased by the blood of the Lamb.

Counterfeit vs. Real 57

In addition to the renunciations listed on the previous page, all other satanic rituals, covenants (promises, contracts, agreements or vows), and assignments must be renounced. Pray and ask the Lord to bring to your remembrance anything else that you need to deal with. Specifically renounce those things the Lord brings to your mind. When finished, complete the following prayer and declaration.

In the Name and authority of the Lord Jesus Christ, I renounce every Satanic sexual ritual and dedication, covenant, and perverted sexual act that was performed over me and done to me. Lord, I renounce my participation, either willingly or unwillingly, in these sinful perverted practices and deeds, and I ask that You please forgive me. Thank you Lord for your forgiveness and cleansing from all unrighteousness. I now receive your forgiveness and cleansing, and I choose in faith to forgive myself. I now command every demon that may have an assignment against me and an attachment to me and these sinful deeds, to leave my presence at once and never return.

> **Five smooth stones that will down the enemy:**
>
> **Christ is.
> Christ can.
> Christ has.
> Christ will.
> Christ does.**

Lord Jesus, I ask You to please take back all of the ground that was given to Satan through these sinful practices and deeds, and that You break all of my bondages to sin and Satan. I also ask that You please heal me of all my wounds, shame and painful memories. Thank you, Lord Jesus.

I announce that by the shed blood of Jesus Christ, I am washed and cleansed of all unrighteousness by the blood of Christ as a result of my participation in Satanic sexual dedications, rituals, covenants, and perverted sexual acts. Therefore, standing firm in this truth, I now declare that I am totally free and clean before my Lord. Thank you Lord Jesus, Amen. (Prayer used by permission Trinity Complete In Christ)

Date _____

Some people who have been subjected to Satanic Ritual Abuse (SRA) develop multiple personalities (alters) in order to cope with their pain. If this is true in your case, you need someone who understands spiritual conflict to help you work through this problem.

Eventually, every alter personality (if this is the case with you), must be identified and guided into resolving the issues that caused its formation. Then, all true alters can agree to come together in Christ. God's Word is true and we need to accept His truth in the innermost part of our being (Ps. 51:6). Whether or not we feel it is true, we need to *believe* it is true!

58   *Counterfeit vs. Real*

Deception vs. Truth

DECEPTION VS. TRUTH

Since Jesus is the truth (Jn. 14:6), the Holy Spirit is the Spirit of truth (Jn. 16:13), and the Word of God is truth (Jn. 17:17), we ought to speak the truth in love (Eph. 4:15).

The believer in Christ has no business deceiving others by lying, exaggerating, telling white lies, stretching the truth or anything relating to falsehoods. Satan is the father of lies (John 8:44), and he seeks to keep us in bondage through deception (Rev. 12:9; 2 Tim. 2:26), but it is the truth that sets us free (Jn. 8:32-36).

We will find real joy and freedom when we stop living a lie and walk openly in the truth. After confessing his sin, King David wrote, "How blessed [happy] is the man... in whose spirit there is no deceit" (Ps. 32:2).

> **We will find real joy and freedom when we stop living a lie and walk openly in the truth.**

How can we find the strength to walk in the light (1 Jn. 1:7)? When we are sure that God loves and accepts us, we can be free to own up to our sin, face reality, and not run and hide from painful circumstances.

Start this step by praying the following prayer out loud. Don't let any opposing thoughts, such as, "This is a waste of time," or "I wish I could believe this stuff but I just can't," keep you from praying and choosing the truth. Even if this is difficult for you, work your way through this step. God will strengthen you as you rely on Him.

Dear Heavenly Father, I know that You want me to know the truth, believe the truth, speak the truth and live in accordance with the truth. Thank You that it is the truth that will set me free.

In many ways I have been deceived by Satan, the father of lies, and I have deceived myself as well. Father, I pray in the name of the Lord Jesus Christ, by virtue of His shed blood and resurrection, asking You to rebuke all of Satan's demons that are deceiving me.

I have trusted in Jesus alone to save me, and so I am Your forgiven child. Therefore, since You accept me just as I am in Christ, I can be free to face my sin and not try to hide. I ask for the Holy Spirit to guide me into all truth. I ask You to "search me, O God, and know my heart; try me and know my anxious thoughts; and see if there be any hurtful way in me, and lead me in the everlasting way" (Ps. 139:23, 24). **In the name of Jesus, Who is the Truth, I pray. Amen.**

There are many ways in which Satan, "the god of this world" (2 Cor. 4:4), seeks to deceive us. Just as he did with Eve, the devil tries to convince us to rely on ourselves. He tempts us to try to get our needs met thru the world around us, rather than by trusting in the provision of our heavenly Father.

60 *Deception vs. Truth*

The following exercise will help open your eyes to the ways you have been deceived by the world system around you. Check each area of deception that the Lord brings to your mind and confess it, using the prayer following the list.

Ways you can be deceived by the world:

❑ Believing that acquiring money and things will bring lasting happiness (Matt. 13:22; 1 Tim. 6:10)

❑ Believing that consuming food and/or alcohol excessively will make me happy (Prov. 20:1; 23:19-21)

❑ Believing that a great body and personality will get me what I want (Prov. 3 1: 10; 1 Pet. 3:3, 4)

❑ Believing that gratifying sexual lust will bring lasting satisfaction (Eph. 4:22; 1 Pet. 2:11)

❑ Believing that I can sin and get away with it and not have it affect my heart (Heb. 3:12, 13)

❑ Believing that I need more than what God has given me in Christ (2 Cor. 11:2-4, 13-15)

❑ Believing that I can do whatever I want and no one can touch me (Prov. 16:18; 1 Pet. 5:5)

❑ Believing that my experience and what I think is more important than what God's word says (1 Cor. 3:18-20)

❑ Believing that I can hang around bad company and not be corrupted (1 Cor. 15:33, 34)

❑ Believing that there are no consequences on earth for my sin (Gal. 6:7, 8)

❑ Believing that I must gain the approval of certain other people in order to be happy (Gal. 1:10)

❑ Believing that I must measure up to certain standards in order to feel good about myself (Gal. 3:2-3; 5:1)

> The devil tempts us to try to get our needs met through the world around us, rather than by trusting in the provision of our heavenly Father.

Lord, I confess that I have been deceived by _____ _____. **I thank You for Your forgiveness, and I commit myself to believing only Your truth. In Jesus name, Amen.**

Deception vs. Truth 61

It is important to know that in addition to being deceived by the world and deceiving spirits, we can also deceive ourselves. Now that you are alive in Christ, completely forgiven and totally accepted, you don't need to defend yourself the way you used to. Christ is now your defense. Confess the ways the Lord shows you that you have deceived yourself or defended yourself wrongly by using the lists and prayers of confession below:

Ways you can deceive yourself:

> Now that you are alive in Christ, completely forgiven, and totally accepted, you don't need to defend yourself the way you used to. Christ is now your defense.

❑ Hearing God's Word but not doing what it says (Jas. 1:22)

❑ Saying I have no sin (1 Jn. 1:8)

❑ Thinking I am something I'm really not (Gal. 6:3)

❑ Thinking I am wise in this worldly age (1 Cor. 3:18, 19)

❑ Thinking I can be truly religious but not bridle my tongue (Jas. 1:26)

Lord, I confess that I have deceived myself by _____. Thank You for Your forgiveness. I commit myself to believing only Your truth. In Jesus' name, Amen.

Ways you can wrongly defend yourself:

❑ Denial of reality (conscious or unconscious)

❑ Fantasy (escaping reality by daydreaming, TV, movies, music, computer or video games, etc.)

❑ Emotional insulation (withdrawing from people or keeping people at a distance to avoid rejection)

❑ Regression (reverting back to a less threatening time)

❑ Displaced anger (taking out my frustrations on innocent people)

❑ Projection (blaming others for my problems)

❑ Rationalization (making excuses for my own poor behavior)

Lord, I confess that I have defended myself wrongly by _____. Thank You for Your forgiveness. I now commit myself to trusting in You to defend and protect me. In Jesus' name, Amen.

Choosing the truth may be hard for you if you have been believing lies for many years. You may need some ongoing counseling to help weed out any defense mechanisms that you have relied on to cope with life. Every Christian needs to learn that Christ is the only defense he or she needs. Realizing that you are already forgiven and accepted by God through Christ will help free you to place all your dependence on Him.

Faith is the biblical response to the truth, and believing what God says is a choice we can all make.

Faith is the biblical response to the truth, and believing what God says is a choice we can all make. If you say, "I wish I could believe God, but I just can't," you are being deceived. Of course you can believe God because what God says is always true.

Sometimes we are greatly hindered from walking by faith in our Father God because of lies we have believed about Him. We are to have a healthy fear of God (awe of His holiness, power and presence), but we are not to be afraid of Him. Romans 8:15 says, "For you have not received a spirit of slavery leading to fear again, but you have received a spirit of adoption as sons by which we cry out, 'Abba! Father!'" The exercise below will help break the chains of those lies and enable you to begin to experience an intimate relationship with your Father God.

Work your way down the lists, one-by-one, left to right. Begin each one with the statement in *large print* at the top of that list. Read through the lists *out loud.*

I renounce the lie that my Father God is...

1. distant and disinterested

2. insensitive and uncaring

3. stern and demanding

4. passive and cold

5. absent or too busy for me

6. never satisfied with what I do, impatient or angry

7. mean, cruel or abusive

8. trying to take all the fun out of life

I joyfully accept the truth that my Father God is...

1. intimate and involved (Ps. 139:1-18)

2. kind and compassionate (Ps. 103:8-14)

3. accepting and filled with joy and love (Rom. 15:7; Zeph. 3:17)

4. warm and affectionate (Is. 40:11; Hos. 11:3-4)

5. always with me and eager to be with me (Heb. 13:5; Jer. 31:20; Ezek. 34:11-16)

6. patient and slow to anger (Exod. 34:6; 2 Pet. 3:9)

7. loving, gentle and protective of me (Jer. 31:3; Is. 42:3; Ps. 18:2)

8. trustworthy and wants to give me a full life; His will is good, perfect and acceptable for me (Lam. 3:22-23; Jn. 10:10; Rom. 12:1-2)

Deception vs. Truth 63

I renounce the lie that my Father God is...	*I joyfully accept the truth that my Father God is...*
9. controlling or manipulative	9. full of grace and mercy, and He gives me freedom to fail (Heb. 4:15-16; Lk. 15:11-16)
10. condemning or unforgiving	10. tender-hearted and forgiving; His heart and arms are always open to me (Ps. 130:1-4; Lk. 15:17-24)
11. nit-picking, exacting or perfectionistic	11. committed to my growth and proud of me as His growing child (Rom. 8:28-29; Heb. 12:5-11; 2 Cor. 7:4)

Just as a lion's roar strikes terror into the hearts of those who hear it, so Satan uses fear to try to paralyze Christians.

A central part of walking in the truth and rejecting deception is to deal with the fears that plague our lives. 1 Peter 5:8 says that our enemy, the devil, prowls around like a roaring lion, seeking people to devour. Just as a lion's roar strikes terror into the hearts of those who hear it, so Satan uses fear to try to paralyze Christians. His intimidation tactics are designed to rob us of faith in God and drive us to try to get our needs met through the world or the flesh.

Fear weakens us, causes us to be self-centered, and clouds our minds so that all we can think about is the thing that frightens us. But fear can only control us if we let it.

God, however, does not want us to be mastered by anything, including fear (1 Cor. 6:12). Jesus Christ is to be our only Master (2 Tim. 2:21; Jn. 13:13). In order to begin to experience freedom from the bondage of fear and the ability to walk by faith in God, pray the following prayer from your heart:

Dear Heavenly Father, I confess to You that I have listened to the devil's roar and have allowed fear to master me. I have not always walked by faith in You but instead have focused on my feelings and circumstances (2 Cor. 4:16-18; 5:7)**. Thank You for forgiving me for my unbelief. Right now I renounce the spirit of fear and affirm the truth that You have not given me a spirit of fear but of power, love and a sound mind** (2 Tim. 1:7)**. Lord, please reveal to my mind now all the fears that have been controlling me so I can renounce them and be free to walk by faith in You.**

I thank You for the freedom You give me to walk by faith and not by fear. In Jesus' powerful name, I pray. Amen.

The following list may help you recognize some of the fears the devil has used to keep you from walking by faith. Check the ones that apply to your life. Write down any others that the Spirit of God brings to your mind. Then, one by one, renounce those fears out loud, using the suggested renunciation below:

Every time you overcome fear, you grow as a person.

- ❏ Fear of death
- ❏ Fear of not being loved by God
- ❏ Fear of Satan
- ❏ Fear of never loving or being loved by others
- ❏ Fear of failure
- ❏ Fear of embarrassment
- ❏ Fear of rejection by people
- ❏ Fear of being victimized by crime
- ❏ Fear of disapproval
- ❏ Fear of marriage
- ❏ Fear of becoming / being homosexual
- ❏ Fear of divorce
- ❏ Fear of financial problems
- ❏ Fear of going crazy
- ❏ Fear of never getting married
- ❏ Fear of pain / illness
- ❏ Fear of the death of a loved one
- ❏ Fear of the future
- ❏ Fear of being a hopeless case
- ❏ Fear of confrontation
- ❏ Fear of losing my salvation
- ❏ Fear of specific individuals (list them)
- ❏ Fear of having committed the unpardonable sin
- ❏ Other specific fears that come to mind now (list them)

I renounce the (name the fear) **because God has not given me a spirit of fear** (2 Tim. 1:7). **I choose to live by faith in the God who has promised to protect me and meet all my needs as I walk by faith in Him** (Ps. 27:1; Matt. 6:33, 34).

Deception vs. Truth 65

After you have finished renouncing all the specific fears you have allowed to control you, pray the following prayer from your heart:

Dear Heavenly Father, I thank You that You are trustworthy. I choose to believe You, even when my feelings and circumstances tell me to fear. You have told me not to fear, for You are with me; not to anxiously look about me, for You are my God. You will strengthen me, help me and surely uphold me with Your righteous right hand (Is. 41:10). **I pray this with faith in the name of Jesus my Master. Amen.**

> **Faith is choosing to believe and act upon what God says, regardless of feelings or circumstances.**

Faith is choosing to believe and act upon what God says, regardless of feelings or circumstances. Believing something, however, does not make it true. *It's true; therefore, we choose to believe it.*

The New Age movement has twisted the concept of faith by saying that we make something true by believing it. No, we can't create reality with our minds; only God can do that. We can only *face* reality with our minds.

Just "having faith" is not enough. The key question is whether the object of your faith is trustworthy. If the object of your faith is not reliable, then no amount of believing will change it. That is why our faith must be on the solid rock of God Himself and His Word. That is the only way to live a responsible and fruitful life. On the other hand, if what you believe in is not true, then how you end up living will not be right.

For generations, Christians have known the importance of publicly declaring what they believe. Read aloud the following "Statement of Truth," thinking about what you are saying. You may find it very helpful to read it daily for several weeks to renew your mind with the truth and replace any lies you may believe.

Statement of Truth

> **For generations, Christians have known the importance of publicly declaring what they believe.**

1. I recognize that there is only one true and living God (Exod. 20:2, 3) who exists as the Father, Son, and Holy Spirit. He is worthy of all honor, praise, and glory as the One Who made all things and holds all things together (Col. 1:16, 17).

2. I recognize that Jesus Christ is the Messiah, the Word Who became flesh and dwelt among us (Jn. 1:1, 14). I believe that He came to destroy the works of the devil (1 Jn. 3:8), and that He disarmed the rulers and authorities and made a public display of them, having triumphed over them (Col. 2:15).

3. I believe that God demonstrated His own love for me in that while I was still a sinner, Christ died for me (Rom. 5:8). I believe that He has

delivered me from the domain of darkness and transferred me to His kingdom, and in Him I have redemption, the forgiveness of sins (Col. 1:13, 14).

> **What you believe (or disbelieve) determines what you do.**
> Mike Quarles

4. I believe that I am now a child of God (1 Jn. 3:1-3) and that I am seated with Christ in the heavenlies (Eph. 2:6). I believe that I was saved by the grace of God through faith and that it was a gift and not a result of any works on my part (Eph. 2:8, 9).

5. I choose to be strong in the Lord and in the strength of His might (Eph. 6:10). I put no confidence in the flesh (Phil. 3:3), for the weapons of warfare are not of the flesh but are divinely powerful for the destruction of strongholds (2 Cor. 10:4). I put on the full armor of God (Eph. 6:10-20). I resolve to stand firm in my faith and resist the evil one.

6. I believe that apart from Christ I can do nothing (Jn. 15:5), so I declare my complete dependence on Him. I choose to abide in Christ in order to bear much fruit and glorify my Father (Jn. 15:8). I announce to Satan that Jesus is my Lord (1 Cor. 12:3), and I reject any and all counterfeit gifts or works of Satan in my life.

7. I believe that the truth will set me free (Jn. 8:32) and that Jesus is the truth (John 14:6). If *He* sets me free, I will be free indeed (Jn. 8:36). I recognize that walking in the light is the only path of true fellowship with God and man (1 Jn. 1:3-7). Therefore, I stand against all of Satan's deception by taking every thought captive in obedience to Christ (2 Cor.10:5). I declare that the Bible is the only authoritative standard for truth and life (2 Tim. 3:15-17).

8. I choose to present my body to God as a living and holy sacrifice (Rom. 12:1) and the members of my body as instruments of righteousness to God (Rom. 6:13). I choose to renew my mind by the living Word of God in order that I may prove that the will of God is good, acceptable and perfect (Rom. 12:2). I put off the old self with its evil practices and put on the new self (Col. 3:9, 10). I declare myself to be a new creation in Christ (2 Cor. 5:17 NIV).

> **Faith makes change possible, not easy.**

9. By faith, I choose to be filled with the Spirit (Eph. 5:18) so that I can be guided into all truth (Jn. 16:13). I choose to walk by the Spirit so that I will not carry out the desires of the flesh (Gal. 5:16).

10. I renounce all selfish goals and choose the ultimate goal of love (1 Tim. 1:5). I choose to obey the two greatest commandments: to love the Lord my God with all my heart, soul, mind, and strength and to love my neighbor as myself (Matt. 22:37-39).

11. I believe that the Lord Jesus has all authority in heaven and on earth (Matt. 28:18) and that He is the head over all rule and authority. I am complete in Him (Col. 2:10). I believe that Satan and his demons are subject to me in Christ since I am a member of Christ's body (Eph. 1:19-23). Therefore, I obey the command to submit to God and resist the devil (Jas. 4:7), and I command Satan in the name of Jesus Christ to leave my presence.

Deception vs. Truth 67

Notes

Defensiveness
is defenseless!

If wrong, you
have no de-
fense; if right,
you need none.

Bitterness vs. Forgiveness

THE THIRD STEP

BITTERNESS VS. FORGIVENESS

We need to forgive others so Satan cannot take advantage of us (2 Cor. 2: 10, 11). We are commanded to get rid of all bitterness in our lives and forgive others as we have been forgiven (Eph. 4:31, 32). Ask God to bring to your mind the people you need to forgive by praying the following prayer out loud:

Dear Heavenly Father, I thank You for the riches of Your kindness, and patience toward me, knowing that Your kindness has led me to repentance (Rom. 2:4). **I confess that I have not shown that same kindness and patience toward those who have hurt me. Instead, I have held on to my anger, bitterness and resentment toward them. Please bring to my mind all the people I need to forgive in order that I may do so now. In Jesus' name, Amen.**

On a separate sheet of paper, list the names of people who come to your mind. At this point don't question whether you need to forgive them or not. If a name comes to mind, just write it down.

Often we hold things against ourselves as well, punishing ourselves for wrong choices we've made in the past. Write "myself" at the bottom of your list so you can forgive yourself. Forgiving yourself is accepting the truth that God has already forgiven you in Christ. If God forgives you, you *can* forgive yourself!

Also write down "thoughts against God" at the bottom of your list. Obviously, God has never done anything wrong so we don't need to forgive Him. Sometimes, however, we harbor angry thoughts against Him because He did not do what we wanted Him to do. Those feelings of anger or resentment against God can become a wall between us and Him, so we must let them go.

> Forgiveness is a choice, a decision of your will. Since God requires you to forgive, it is something you *can* do.

After making your list, take a few minutes to review what forgiveness is and what it is not.

Forgiveness is not forgetting. People who want to forget all that was done to them will find they cannot do it. Don't put off forgiving those who have hurt you, hoping the pain will one day go away. Once you choose to forgive someone, *then* Christ can come and begin to heal you of your hurts. But the healing cannot begin until you first forgive.

Forgiveness is a choice, a decision of your will. Since God requires you to forgive, it is something you can do. Sometimes it is very hard to forgive someone because we naturally want revenge for the things we have suffered. Forgiveness seems to go against our sense of what is right and fair. So we hold on to our anger, punishing people over and over again in our minds for the pain they've caused us.

But we are told by God never to take our own revenge (Rom. 12:19). Let God deal with the person. Let them off your hook because as long as you refuse to forgive someone, you are still hooked to them. You are still chained to your past, bound up in your bitterness.

By forgiving, you let the other person off of your hook, but they are not off God's hook. You must trust that God will deal with the person justly and fairly, something you simply cannot do.

You might say, "But you don't know how much this person hurt me!" You're right. We don't, but Jesus does, and He tells you to forgive. And don't you see? Until you let go of your anger and hatred, the person is still hurting you. You can't turn back the clock and change the past, but you can be free from it. You *can* stop the pain, but there is only one way to do it—forgive.

> *Do not wait for the other person to ask for forgiveness before forgiving them.*

God wants you to be free. Forgiveness is mainly a matter of obedience to Him. You forgive others so you can be free; there is no other way.

Forgiveness is agreeing to live with the consequences of another person's sin, but you are going to live with those consequences anyway whether you like it or not. The only choice you have is whether you will do so in the *bondage of bitterness or in the freedom of forgiveness.*

But no one truly forgives without accepting and suffering the pain of another person's sin. That can seem unfair and you may wonder where the justice is. Justice is found at the cross which makes forgiveness legally and morally right.

Jesus took the *eternal* consequences of sin upon Himself. God "made Him who knew no sin to be sin on our behalf, that we might become the righteousness of God in Him" (2 Cor. 5:21). We, however, often suffer the temporary consequences of other people's sins. This is simply a harsh reality of life that all of us have to face.

Do not wait for the other person to ask for your forgiveness before forgiving them. They may never do so. Remember, Jesus did not wait for those who were crucifying Him to apologize before He forgave them. Even while they mocked and jeered at Him, He prayed, "Father, forgive them, for they know not what they do" (Lk. 23:34).

> *Forgiveness is choosing not to hold someone's sin against him or her any more.*

How do you forgive from your heart? You allow God to bring to the surface the painful emotions you feel toward those who've hurt you. If your forgiveness doesn't touch the emotional core of your life, it will be incomplete. Too often we're afraid of the pain, so we bury our emotions deep down inside us. Let God bring them to the surface so that He can begin to heal those damaged emotions.

Forgiveness is choosing not to hold a person's sin against him or her anymore. It is common for bitter people to bring up past issues with those who have hurt them. They want them to feel bad. But we must let go of the past and choose to reject any thought of revenge.

Bitterness vs. Forgiveness **71**

past and choose to reject any thought of revenge.

This doesn't mean you must continue to put up with the future sins of others. God does not tolerate sin and neither should you. Don't allow yourself to be continually abused by others. Take a stand against sin while continuing to exercise grace and forgiveness toward those who hurt you. You may need help in setting wise limits and boundaries to protect yourself from further abuse.

Don't wait to forgive until you feel like forgiving. You will never get there. Make the hard choice to forgive even if you don't feel like it. Once you choose to forgive, Satan will have lost his power over you in that area, and God's healing touch will be free to move. **Freedom is what you will gain right now, not necessarily an immediate change in feelings.**

Make the hard choice to forgive even if you don't feel like it.

Now you are ready to begin. Starting with the first person on your list, make the choice to forgive him or her for every painful memory that comes to your mind. Stay with that individual until you are sure you have dealt with all the remembered pain. Then work your way down the list, dealing with each person in the same manner.

As you begin forgiving people, God may bring to your mind painful memories you've totally forgotten. Let Him do this even if it hurts. God wants you to be free; forgiving these people is the only way. Don't try to excuse the offender's behavior, even if it is someone you are really close to. Don't say, "Lord, please help me to forgive." He is already helping you and will be with you all the way through the process. Don't say, "Lord, I want to forgive..." because that bypasses the hard choice we have to make. Say, "Lord, I *choose* to forgive..."

For every painful memory you have concerning each person on your list, pray out loud:

Lord, I choose to forgive (name the person) **for** (say what they did to hurt you) **even though it made me feel** (express the feelings on the opposite page which apply).

Once you choose to forgive, Satan will have lost his power over you in that area.

After you have forgiven each person for all the offenses that came to your mind, and after you have honestly expressed how you felt, conclude your forgiveness of that person by praying out loud:

Lord, I choose not to hold any of these things against (name) **any longer. I thank You for setting me free from the bondage of my bitterness toward** (name). **I ask You to bless** (name) **as you see fit. In Jesus' name, I pray. Amen.**

To forgive from the heart, you must acknowledge your feelings.

abandoned	exhausted	nervous
accused	failure	out of control
afraid	fearful	overprotected
alone	frustrated	overwhelmed
angry	furious	rejected
annoyed	guilty	resentful
anxious	harassed	sad
ashamed	hateful	shamed
bad	helpless	stupid
betrayed	hopeless	tense
bitter	hurt	threatened
bothered	inadequate	trapped
condemned	inferior	troubled
confused	ignored	unclean
defeated	irritated	unloved
depressed	insecure	unprotected
devastated	jealous	used
dirty	judged	unwanted
disappointed	lonely	uptight
discouraged	lost	victimized
disgusted	miserable	violated
distressed	misunderstood	worried
dumb	mixed up	worthless
embarrassed	neglected	other _____

Notes

Bitterness vs. Forgiveness

Notes

The doorway that
opens to a life of
love and joy is
forgiveness.
Brian Tracy

Rebellion vs. Submission

REBELLION VS. SUBMISSION

We live in a rebellious age. Many people only obey laws and authorities when it is convenient for them. There is a general lack of respect for those in government, and Christians are often as guilty as the rest of society in fostering a critical, rebellious spirit. Certainly, we are not expected to agree with our leaders' policies which are in violation of Scripture, but we are to "honor all men, love the brotherhood, fear God, honor the king" (1 Pet. 2:17).

It is easy to believe the lie that those in authority over us are only robbing us of the freedom to do what we want. The truth is, however, that God has placed them there for our protection and liberty.

Rebelling against God and His authorities gives Satan a wide open avenue to attack.

Rebelling against God and His authorities is a very serious sin for it gives Satan a wide open avenue to attack. Submission is the only solution. God requires more, however, than just the outward appearance of submission; He wants us to sincerely submit to those in authority from the heart. When you stand under the authority of God and those He has placed over you, you cut off this dangerous avenue of demonic attack.

We have two biblical responsibilities regarding authority figures: Pray for them and submit to them (1 Tim. 2:1-2; Rom. 13:1-7). The only time God permits us to disobey earthly leaders is when they require us to do something morally wrong before God or attempt to rule outside the realm of their authority. Pray the following prayer:

Dear Heavenly Father, You have said in the Bible that rebellion is the same thing as witchcraft and as bad as idolatry (1 Sam. 15:23)**. I know I have not obeyed You in this area and have rebelled in my heart against You and against those You have placed in authority over me. Thank You for Your forgiveness of my rebellion. By the shed blood of the Lord Jesus Christ, I pray that all ground gained by evil spirits in my life due to my rebellion would be canceled. I pray that You would show me all the ways I have been rebellious. I choose now to adopt a submissive spirit and a servant's heart. In Jesus' precious name, I pray. Amen.**

God requires more than just the outward appearance of submission.

Being under authority is clearly an act of faith! By submitting, you are trusting God to work through His established lines of authority, even when they are harsh or unkind or when they tell you to do something you don't want to do.

There may be times when those over you abuse their authority and break the laws which are ordained by God for the protection of innocent people. In those cases, you will need to seek help from a higher authority for your protection. The laws in your state may require that such abuse be reported to the police or other governmental agency.

If there is continuing abuse (physical, mental, emotional or sexual) where you live, you may need further counseling help to deal with that situation.

If authorities abuse their position by requiring you to break God's law or compromise your commitment to Him, then you need to obey God rather than man (Acts 4:19, 20). Be careful though. Don't assume that an authority is violating God's Word just because they are telling you to do something you don't like!

We all need to adopt a humble, submissive spirit to one another in the fear of Christ (Eph. 5:21). In addition, however, God has set up specific lines of authority to protect us and give order to our daily lives.

> **God has set up specific lines of authority to protect us and give order to our daily lives.**

As you prayerfully look over the list below, allow the Lord to show you any *specific ways* in which you have been rebellious to authority. Then, using the prayer of confession that follows the list, specifically confess whatever the Lord brings to your mind.

❑ Civil Government (including traffic laws, tax laws, attitude toward government officials) (Rom. 13:1-7; 1 Tim. 2:1-4; 1 Pet. 2:13-17)

❑ Parents, Stepparents or Legal Guardians (Eph. 6:1-3)

❑ Teachers, Coaches, School Officials (Rom. 13:1-4)

❑ Employer (past or present) (1 Pet. 2:18-23)

❑ Husband (1 Pet. 3:1-4) or Wife (Eph. 5:21; 1 Pet. 3:7)
[**Note to Husbands**: Take a moment, and ask the Lord if your lack of Christ-like love for your wife could be fostering a rebellious spirit within her. If so, confess your failure now as a violation of Eph. 5:22-33.]

❑ Church Leaders (Heb. 13:7)

❑ God Himself (Dan. 9:5, 9)

For each way in which the Spirit of God brings to your mind that you have been rebellious, use the following prayer to specifically confess that sin:

Lord, I confess that I have been rebellious toward_____ by (say what you did specifically). **Thank You for forgiving my rebellion. I choose now to be submissive and obedient to Your Word. In Jesus' name, I pray. Amen.**

Rebellion vs. Submission 77

> When you know you've got humility, you've lost it. Humility is to make a right estimate of one's self.
> Charles Spurgeon

Notes

Pride vs. Humility

The Fifth Step

PRIDE VS. HUMILITY

Pride kills. Pride says, "I don't need God or anyone else's help. I can handle it by myself." Oh, no you can't! We absolutely need God, and we desperately need each other. The apostle Paul wisely wrote, "We worship in the Spirit of God and glory in Christ Jesus and put *no confidence in the flesh*" (Phil. 3:3).

That is a good definition of humility: putting no confidence in the flesh, that is in ourselves; but rather, being "*strong in the Lord and in the strength of his might*" (Eph. 6: 10). Humility is confidence properly placed—in God.

Proverbs 3:5-7 expresses a similar thought: "Trust in the LORD with all your heart and do not lean on your own understanding. In all your ways acknowledge Him and He will make your paths straight. Do not be wise in your own eyes; fear the LORD and turn away from evil."

James 4: 6-10 and 1 Peter 5:1-10 warn us that serious spiritual problems will result when we are proud. Use the following prayer to express your commitment to living humbly before God:

> **Dear Heavenly Father, You have said that pride goes before destruction and an arrogant spirit before stumbling** (Prov. 16:18)**. I confess that I have been thinking mainly of myself and not of others. I have not denied myself, picked up my cross daily and followed You** (Matt. 16:24)**. As a result, I have given ground to Satan in my life. I have sinned by believing I could be happy and successful on my own. I confess that I have placed my will before Yours and have centered my life around myself instead of You.**
>
> **I repent of my pride and selfishness and pray that all ground gained in my members by the enemies of the Lord Jesus Christ would be canceled. I choose to rely on the Holy Spirit's power and guidance so I will do nothing from selfishness or empty conceit, but with humility of mind I will regard others as more important than myself** (Phil. 2:3)**. And I choose to make You, Lord, the most important of all in my life** (Matt. 6:33)**.**
>
> **Please show me now all the specific ways in which I have lived my life in pride. Enable me through love to serve others and in honor to prefer others** (Rom. 12:10)**. I ask all of this in the gentle and humble name of Jesus, my Lord. Amen.**

Having made that commitment to God in prayer, now allow Him to show you any specific ways in which you have lived pridefully. The following list may help you.

Humility is confidence properly placed —in God.

Serious spiritual problems will result when we are proud.

80 *Pride vs. Humility*

As the Lord brings to your mind areas of pride, use the prayer below to guide you in your confession.

❑ Having a stronger desire to do my will than God's will.

❑ Leaning too much on my own understanding and experience rather than seeking God's guidance through prayer and His Word.

❑ Relying on my own strengths and abilities rather than depending on the power of the Holy Spirit.

❑ Being more concerned about controlling others than developing self-control.

❑ Often being too busy doing "important" things to take time to do little things for others.

❑ Having a tendency to think that I have no needs.

❑ Finding it hard to admit when I am wrong.

❑ Being more concerned about pleasing people than pleasing God.

❑ Thinking I am more humble, spiritual, religious or devoted than others.

❑ Being driven to obtain recognition by attaining degrees, titles or positions.

❑ Being overly concerned about getting the credit I feel I deserve.

❑ Often feeling that my needs are more important than other's.

❑ Considering myself better than others because of my academic, artistic, or athletic abilities or accomplishments.

❑ Other ways I have thought more highly of myself than I should:

_____

_____

> *Outward actions are reflections of inner thoughts.*
> T.W. Hunt;
> Claude W. King

> *Satan's strategy is always to divide and conquer.*

For each of the above areas that has been true in your life, pray out loud:

Lord, I agree I have been prideful in_____. Thank You for forgiving me for my pride. I choose to humble myself before You and others. I choose to place all my confidence in You and none in my flesh. In Jesus' name, Amen.

Pride vs. Humility 81

Pride is the original sin of Lucifer. It sets one person or group against another and divides. Satan's strategy is always to divide and conquer, but God wants to bring us together as one in Christ.

Consider for a moment the work of Christ in breaking down the long-standing barrier of racial prejudice between Jew and Gentile:

"For He Himself [Christ] is our peace, who has made the two one and has destroyed the barrier, the dividing wall of hostility, by abolishing in His flesh the law with its commandments and regulations. His purpose was to create in Himself one new man out of the two, thus making peace, and in this one body to reconcile both of them to God through the cross, by which He put to death their hostility. He came and preached peace to you who were far away and peace to those who were near. For through Him we both have access to the Father by one Spirit" (Eph. 2:14-18 NIV).

Many times we deny that there is prejudice or bigotry in our hearts, yet "nothing in all creation is hidden from God's sight. Everything is uncovered and laid bare before the eyes of Him to whom we must give account" (Heb. 4:13 NIV,). The following prayer asks God to shine His light upon your heart and reveal any area of proud prejudice:

> **Dear Heavenly Father, I know that You love all people equally and that You do not show favoritism but You accept men from every nation who fear You and do what is right** (Acts 10:34). **You do not judge people based on skin color, race, ethnic background, gender, denominational preference or any other worldly matter** (2 Cor. 5:16). **I confess that I have too often prejudged others or regarded myself superior because of these things. I have been a proud agent of division rather than unity through my attitudes, words and deeds. I repent of all bigotry and prejudice, and I ask You, Lord, to now reveal to my mind all the specific ways in which this form of pride has corrupted my heart and mind. In Jesus' name, Amen.**

For each area of racial or ethnic prejudice, gender superiority or denominational bigotry that the Lord brings to mind, pray the following prayer out loud from your heart:

> **Lord, I confess and renounce the prideful sin of prejudice against** (name the group). **I thank You for Your forgiveness. I ask You to change my heart now and make me a loving agent of friendship and fellowship with** (name the group). **In Jesus' name, Amen.**

> "Nothing in all creation is hidden from God's sight. Everything is uncovered and laid bare before the eyes of Him to whom we must give account."
>
> Heb. 4:13

Bondage vs. Freedom

The Sixth Step

BONDAGE VS. FREEDOM

Many times we feel trapped in a vicious cycle of "sin-confess-sin-confess" that never seems to end. We can become very discouraged and end up just giving up and giving in to the sins of our flesh. To find freedom we must follow James 4:7, "Submit therefore to God. Resist the devil and he will flee from you." We submit to God by confession of sin and repentance (turning away from it). We resist the devil by rejecting his lies and walking in the truth.

Sin that has become a habit often requires help from a trusted brother or sister in Christ. James 5:16 says, "Confess your sins to one another and pray for one another so that you may be healed. The effective prayer of a righteous man can accomplish much." Sometimes the assurance of 1 John 1:9 is enough: "If we confess our sins, He is faithful and righteous to forgive us our sins and to cleanse us from all unrighteousness."

Remember, confession is not saying, "I'm sorry"; it is openly admitting, "I did it." Whether you need help from other people or just the accountability of walking in the light before God, pray the following prayer out loud:

> *Remember, confession is not saying, "I'm sorry"; it is openly admitting, "I did it".*

Dear Heavenly Father, You have told me to put on the Lord Jesus Christ and make no provision for the flesh in regard to its lust (Rom. 13:14). **I confess that I have given in to fleshly lusts which wage war against my soul** (1 Pet. 2: 11). **I thank You that in Christ my sins are already forgiven. But I have broken Your holy law and given the devil a chance to wage war in my body** (Rom. 6:12, 13; Jas. 4:1; 1 Pet. 5:8). **I come to You now to confess and renounce these sins of the flesh** (Prov. 28.13; 2 Cor. 4:2) **so that I might be cleansed and set free from the bondage of sin. Please reveal to my mind now all the sins of the flesh I have committed and the ways I have grieved the Holy Spirit. In Jesus' holy name, I pray. Amen.**

There are many sins of the flesh that can control us. The list to follow contains many of them, but a prayerful examination of Galatians 5:19-21, Mark 7:20-23 and other Scripture passages will help you be even more thorough.

Look over the list on the opposite page, and ask the Holy Spirit to bring to your mind the ones you need to confess. He may reveal to you others as well. For each one the Lord shows you, pray a prayer of confession from your heart. There is a sample prayer following the list. Note: Sexual sins, divorce, eating disorders, substance abuse, abortion, suicidal tendencies, and perfectionism will be dealt with later in this step.

> *"If we confess our sins, He is faithful and just and will forgive us our sins and purify us from all unrighteousness."*
> 1 John 1:9

❑	Stealing	❑	Swearing
❑	Quarreling / Fighting	❑	Drug Abuse
❑	Apathy / Laziness	❑	Cheating
❑	Jealousy / Envy	❑	Lying
❑	Procrastination	❑	Complaining / Criticism
❑	Hatred	❑	Greed / Materialism
❑	Lusting	❑	Anger / Bitterness
❑	Gossip / Slander	❑	Verbal Abuse / Railing
❑	Drunkenness	❑	Emotional Abuse / Neglect
❑	Gluttony	❑	Physical Abuse / Cruelty
❑	Controlling	❑	Other _____

> Christian living is not our living with Christ's help, it is Christ living His life in us.
>
> J. E. Conant

Lord, I confess that I have committed the sin of _____ _____. It makes me sad to realize how I have grieved You and hurt the people around me. Thank You for Your forgiveness and cleansing. I now turn away from this sin and turn to You, Lord. Strengthen me by Your Holy Spirit to obey You. In Jesus' name, Amen.

It is our responsibility not to allow sin to have control over our bodies. We must not use our bodies or another person's body as an instrument of unrighteousness (Rom. 6:12, 13). Sexual immorality is sin against your body, the temple of the Holy Spirit (1 Cor. 6:18-19). To find freedom from sexual bondage, begin by praying the following prayer:

Lord, I ask You to bring to my mind every sexual use of my body as an instrument of unrighteousness, so I can renounce these sins right now. In Jesus' name, I pray. Amen.

As the Lord brings to your mind every wrong sexual use of your body, whether it was done to you (rape, incest, sexual molestation) or willingly by you, (sexual immorality) renounce every occasion: (Pornography will be addressed under "Special Prayers for Special Needs".)

Lord, I renounce (name the specific misuse of your body) **with** (name the person) **and I ask You to break that sinful bond.**

Bondage vs. Freedom 85

After you are finished, commit your body to the Lord by praying:

> **Lord, I renounce all these uses of my body as an instrument of unrighteousness, and I confess my participation. I choose now to present my eyes, mouth, mind, heart, hands, feet and sexual organs to You as instruments of righteousness. I present my whole body to You as a living sacrifice, holy and acceptable, and I choose to reserve the sexual use of my body for marriage only** (Heb. 13:4)**.**
>
> **I reject the devil's lie that my body is dirty or in any way unacceptable to You as a result of my past sexual experiences. Lord, thank You that You have totally cleansed and forgiven me and that You love and accept me just the way I am. Therefore, I choose now to accept myself and my body as clean in Your eyes. Amen.**

God will only do as much for us as we allow Him to do in us.

Special Prayers for Special Needs

Pornography

> **Lord, I confess that I have used the members of my body as instruments of unrighteousness in viewing and lusting after pornographic, sexually explicit materials; by indulging in the sexual fantasies in my mind; and through masturbation for my own satisfaction and pleasure. Lord, I also confess that I have participated in and used the following things to stimulate my lustful passions and desires for sex:**

❏ Sexual Fantasies   ❏ Porn Books, Magazines, etc.
❏ Movies and Television   ❏ The Internet
❏ Pictures   ❏ Voyeurism (window peeping, etc.)
❏ Books (romance, sex novels)   ❏ Other _____

Recovery requires personal application of God's Word but not continual focus on self.

> **In the Name and authority of my Lord Jesus Christ, I renounce my participation in the sin of pornography and masturbation, and I ask your forgiveness for sinning against You and against my own body. Thank you Lord for forgiving me. I receive your forgiveness and cleansing, and I choose in faith to forgive myself. I now command every demon that may have an assignment against me and an attachment to me and these sinful deeds, to leave my presence at once and never return.**
>
> **Lord Jesus, I ask that You please take back all of the ground that I have given to Satan through my deeds of unrighteousness and break all of my bondages to these sins and Satan. Please wash and cleanse my mind, will, emotions, memory and body of all unrighteousness. Thank you Jesus, Amen.** (Prayer used by permission, Trinity Complete In Christ Ministries)

86   *Bondage vs. Freedom*

Divorce

Lord, I confess to You any part that I played in my divorce (ask the Lord to show you specifics). **Thank You for Your forgiveness and I choose to forgive myself as well. I renounce the lie that my identity is now in "being divorced." I am a child of God, and I reject the lie that says I am a second-class Christian because of the divorce. I reject the lie that says I am worthless, unlovable, and that my life is empty and meaningless. I am complete in Christ Who loves me and accepts me just as I am. Lord, I commit the healing of all hurts in my life to You as I have chosen to forgive those who have hurt me. I also place my future into Your hands and trust You to provide the human companionship You created me to need through Your church and, if it be Your will, through another spouse. I pray all this in the healing name of Jesus, my Savior, Lord and closest friend. Amen.**

> *Fear is in the darkroom where Satan develops his negatives.*

Homosexuality

Lord, I renounce the lie that You have created me or anyone else to be homosexual. I agree that in Your Word You clearly forbid homosexual behavior. I choose to accept myself as a child of God, and I thank You that You created me as a man (woman). **I renounce all homosexual thoughts, urges, drives and acts, and cancel out all ways that Satan has used these things to pervert my relationships. I announce that I am free in Christ to relate to the opposite sex and my own sex in the way that You intended. In Jesus' name, Amen.**

Abortion

Lord, I confess that I was not a proper guardian and keeper of the life You entrusted to me, and I admit that as sin. Thank You that because of Your forgiveness, I can forgive myself. I recognize that the child is in Your caring hands for all eternity. In Jesus' name, Amen.

Suicidal Tendencies

> *Since we mean so much to God, we would hurt Him deeply if we destroyed ourselves.*

Lord, I renounce all suicidal thoughts and any attempts I've made to take my own life or in any way injure myself. I renounce the lie that life is hopeless and that I can find peace and freedom by taking my own life. Satan is a thief and comes to steal, kill and destroy. I choose life in Christ Who said He came to give me life and give it abundantly (John 10:10). **Thank You for Your forgiveness which allows me to forgive myself. I choose to believe that there is always hope in Christ. In Jesus' name, I pray. Amen.**

Bondage vs. Freedom

Drivenness and Perfectionism

Lord, I renounce the lie that my self-worth is dependent upon my ability to perform. I announce the truth that my identity and sense of worth is found in who I am as Your child. I renounce seeking the approval and acceptance of other people. I choose to believe that I am already approved and accepted in Christ because of His death and resurrection for me. I choose to believe the truth that I have been saved, not by righteous deeds, but by Your mercy. I choose to believe that I am no longer under the curse of the law because Christ became a curse for me. I receive the free gift of life in Christ and choose to abide in Him. I renounce striving for perfection by living under the law. By Your grace, Heavenly Father, I choose from this day forward to walk by faith in the power of Your Holy Spirit. In Jesus' name, Amen.

Eating Disorders or Self-mutilation

Freedom and disobedience to God do not mix.

Lord, I renounce the lie that my value as a person depends upon my appearance or performance. I renounce cutting or abusing myself, vomiting, using laxatives or starving myself as a means of being in control, altering my appearance or cleansing myself of evil. I announce that only the blood of the Lord Jesus cleanses me from sin. I realize I have been bought with a price and my body, the temple of the Holy Spirit, belongs to God. Therefore, I choose to glorify God in my body. I renounce the lie that I am evil or that my body is evil. Thank You that You accept me just the way I am in Christ. In Jesus' name I pray. Amen.

Substance Abuse

Lord, I confess that I have misused substances (alcohol, tobacco, food, prescription or street drugs) **for the purpose of pleasure, to escape reality, or to cope with difficult problems. I confess that I have abused my body and programmed my mind in a harmful way. I have quenched the Holy Spirit as well. Thank You for forgiving me. I renounce any satanic connection or influence in my life through my misuse of food or chemicals. I cast my anxieties on Christ Who loves me. I commit myself to no longer yield to substance abuse. Instead, I choose to allow the Holy Spirit to control and empower me. In Jesus' name, Amen.**

After you have confessed all known sin, pray:

"I press on toward the goal to win the prize for which God has called me."
Philippians 3:14

Lord, I now confess these sins to You and claim my forgiveness and cleansing through the blood of the Lord Jesus Christ. I cancel out all ground that evil spirits have gained through my willful involvement in sin. I pray this in the wonderful name of my Lord and Savior, Jesus Christ. Amen.

Curses vs. Blessings

CURSES VS. BLESSINGS

The last step to freedom is to renounce the sins of your ancestors as well as any curses which may have been placed on you by deceived and evil people or groups.

In giving the Ten Commandments, God said, "You shall not make for yourself an idol or any likeness of what is in heaven above or on the earth beneath or in the water under the earth. You shall not worship them or serve them; for I, the LORD your God, am a jealous God, visiting the iniquity of the fathers on the children to the third and fourth generations of those who hate Me but showing loving kindness to thousands, to those who love Me and keep My commandments" (Exod. 20:4-6).

Demonic or familiar spirits can be passed on from one generation to the next if you don't renounce the sins of your ancestors and claim your new spiritual heritage in Christ. You are not guilty for the sin of any ancestor, but because of their sin, Satan may have gained access to your family.

Some problems, of course, are hereditary or acquired from an immoral environment. But some problems are the result of generational sin. All three conditions can contribute toward causing someone to struggle with a particular sin.

Ask the Lord to show you specifically what sins are characteristic of your family by praying the following prayer. Then list those sins in the space provided below.

> **Dear Heavenly Father, I ask You to reveal to my mind now all the sins of my fathers that are being passed down through family lines. I want to be free from those influences and walk in my new identity as a child of God. In Jesus' name, Amen.**

As the Lord brings those areas of family sin to your mind, list them below. You will be specifically renouncing them later in this step.

1. _____
2. _____
3. _____
4. _____
5. _____

6. _____
7. _____
8. _____
9. _____
10. _____

> *If God sends us over rocky paths, He will provide us with sturdy shoes.*
> Maclaren

In order to walk free from the sins of your ancestors and any curses and assignments targeted against you, read the following declaration and pray the following prayer out loud. Remember, you have all the authority and protection you need in Christ to take your stand against such activity.

Declaration

I, here and now, reject and disown all the sins of my ancestors. I specifically renounce the sins of (list here the areas of family sin the Lord revealed to you). **As one who has now been delivered from the domain of darkness into the kingdom of God's Son, I cancel out all demonic working that has been passed down to me from my family. As one who has been crucified and raised with Jesus Christ (and who sits with Him in heavenly places), I renounce all satanic assignments that are directed toward me and my ministry. I cancel out every curse that Satan and his workers have put on me. I announce to Satan and all his forces that Christ became a curse for me when He died for my sins on the cross** (Gal. 3:13). **I reject any and every way in which Satan may claim ownership of me. I belong to the Lord Jesus Christ who purchased me with His own blood. I reject all blood sacrifices whereby Satan may claim ownership of me. I declare myself to be fully and eternally signed over and committed to the Lord Jesus Christ. By the authority I have in Christ, I now command every familiar spirit and every enemy of the Lord Jesus that is influencing me to leave my presence. I commit myself to my Heavenly Father to do His will from this day forward.**

> Knowing that God is within us, whether we feel His presence or not, gives us the power to be an overcomer.
> Marie Schilling

Prayer

Dear Heavenly Father, I come to You as Your child, bought out of slavery to sin by the blood of the Lord Jesus Christ. You are the Lord of the universe and the Lord of my life. I submit my body to You as an instrument of righteousness, a living and holy sacrifice that I may glorify You in my body. I now ask You to fill me with the Holy Spirit. I commit myself to the renewing of my mind in order to prove that Your will is good, acceptable and perfect for me. All this I pray in the name and authority of the risen Lord Jesus Christ. Amen.

Even after finding freedom in Christ by going through these seven steps, you may still be attacked by demonic influences trying to regain control of your mind, hours, days or even weeks later. But you don't have to let Satan take over. As you continue to walk in humble submission to God, you can resist the devil and he *will* flee from you (Jas. 4:7).

Curses vs. Blessings 91

AFTERCARE

The devil is attracted to sin like flies are attracted to garbage.

The devil is attracted to sin like flies are attracted to garbage. Get rid of the garbage and the flies will depart for smellier places. In the same way, walk in the truth, confessing all sin and forgiving those who hurt you, and the devil will have no place in your life to set up shop.

Realize that one victory does not mean the battles are over. Freedom must be maintained. After completing these steps to freedom, one happy lady asked, "Will I always be like this?" I told her she would stay free as long as she remained in right relationship with God. "Even if you slip and fall," I encouraged, "you know how to get right with God again."

One victim of horrible atrocities shared this illustration: "It's like being forced to play a game with an ugly stranger in my own home. I kept losing and wanted to quit but the ugly stranger wouldn't let me. Finally, I called the police (a higher authority) and they came and escorted the stranger out. He knocked on the door trying to regain entry, but this time I recognized his voice and didn't let him in."

What a beautiful picture of gaining and keeping your freedom in Christ! We call upon Jesus, the ultimate authority, and He escorts the enemy of our souls out of our lives.

Your freedom must be maintained. We cannot emphasize that enough. You have won a very important battle in an ongoing war. Freedom will continue to be yours as long as you keep choosing the truth and standing firm in the strength of the Lord.

Freedom must be maintained.

If you become aware of lies you have believed, renounce them and choose the truth. If new, painful memories surface, forgive those who hurt you. If the Lord shows you other areas of sin in your life, confess those promptly. This tool can serve as a constant guide for you in dealing with the things God points out to you. Some people have found it helpful to walk through the "Steps to Freedom in Christ" again. As you do, follow the instructions carefully.

To maintain your freedom in Christ, we strongly suggest the following as well:

1. Be involved in a loving, caring church fellowship where you can be open and honest with others and where God's truth is taught with grace. Hopefully, the church will sponsor a support group such as Overcomers in Christ to give you a safe place to share and grow.

2. Read and meditate on the Bible daily. Memorize key verses from the "Steps to Freedom in Christ". You may want to read the "Statement of Truth" (pages 38-39) out loud daily and study the verses in it.

3. Learn to take every thought captive to the obedience of Christ. Assume responsibility for your thought life. Don't let your mind become passive. Reject all lies, choose to focus on the truth, and stand firm in your true identity as a child of God in Christ.

Assume responsibility for your thought life.

4. Don't drift back to old patterns of thinking, feeling and acting. This can happen very easily if you become spiritually and mentally lazy. If you are struggling with walking in the truth, share your battles openly with a trusted friend who will pray for you and encourage you to stand firm.

5. Don't expect other people to fight your battles for you, however. They can help you, but they can't think, pray, read the Bible, or choose the truth for you.

6. Commit yourself to daily prayer. Prayer demonstrates a life of trusting in and depending on God. You can pray the following prayers often and with confidence. Let the words come from your heart as well as your lips, and feel free to change them to make our prayers your prayers.

Daily Prayer and Declaration

Dear Heavenly Father, I praise You and honor You as my Lord. You are in control of all things. I thank You that You are always with me and will never leave me nor forsake me. You are the only all-powerful and only wise God. You are kind and loving in all Your ways. I love You and thank You that I am united with Christ and spiritually alive in Him. I choose not to love the world or the things in the world, and I crucify the flesh and all its passions.

Don't expect other people to fight your battles for you.

Thank You for the life I now have in Christ. I ask You to fill me with the Holy Spirit so I may say "no" to sin and "yes" to You. I declare my total dependence upon You, and I take my stand against Satan and all his lying ways. I choose to believe the truth of God's Word despite what my feelings may say. I refuse to be discouraged because You are the God of all hope. Nothing is too difficult for You. I am confident that You will supply all my needs as I seek to live according to Your Word. I thank You that I can be content and live a responsible life through Christ Who strengthens me.

I now take my stand against Satan and command him and all his evil spirits to depart from me. I choose to put on the full armor of God so I may be able to stand firm against all the devil's schemes. I submit my body as a living and holy sacrifice to God, and I choose to renew my mind by the living Word of God. By so doing I will be able to prove that the will of God is good, acceptable and perfect for me. In the name of my Lord and Savior, Jesus Christ, Amen.

Aftercare 93

Bedtime Prayer

Thank You, Lord, that You have brought me into Your family and have blessed me with every spiritual blessing in the heavenly places in Christ Jesus. Thank You for this time of renewal and refreshment through sleep. I accept it as one of Your blessings for Your children, and I trust You to guard my mind and my body during my sleep.

As I have thought about You and Your truth during the day, I choose to let those good thoughts continue in my mind while I am asleep. I commit myself to You for Your protection against every attempt of Satan and his demons to attack me during sleep. Guard my mind from nightmares. I renounce all fear and cast every anxiety upon You, Lord. I commit myself to You as my rock, my fortress and my strong tower. May Your peace be upon this place of rest now. In the strong name of the Lord Jesus Christ, I pray. Amen.

Cleansing Home / Apartment / Room

After removing and destroying all objects of false worship, pray aloud in every room if necessary:

Heavenly Father, I acknowledge that You are the Lord of heaven and earth. In Your sovereign power and love, You have given me all things to richly enjoy. Thank You for this place to live. I claim my home as a place of spiritual safety for me (and my family) and protection from all the attacks of the enemy. As a child of God, raised up and seated with Christ in the heavenly places, I command every evil spirit claiming ground in this place, based on the activities of past or present occupants, including me, to leave and never return. I renounce all curses and spells directed against this place. I ask You, Heavenly Father, to post Your holy, warring angels around this place to guard it from any and all attempts of the enemy to enter and disturb Your purposes for me (and my family). I thank You, Lord, for doing this in the name of the Lord Jesus Christ. Amen.

Living in a Non-Christian Environment

After removing and destroying all objects of false worship from your possession, pray aloud in the place where you live:

Thank You, Heavenly Father, for a place to live and to be renewed by sleep. I ask You to set aside my room (my portion of this room) as a place of spiritual safety for me. I renounce any allegiance given to false gods or spirits by other occupants. I renounce any claim to this room (space) by Satan based on the activities of past or present occupants, including me. On the basis of my position as a child of God and joint-heir with Christ Who has all authority in heaven and on earth, I command all evil spirits to leave this place and never return. I ask You, Heavenly Father, to station Your holy, warring angels to protect me while I live here In Jesus' mighty name, I pray. Amen.

94   *Aftercare*

WHO I AM IN CHRIST

Continue to walk in the truth that your identity and sense of worth comes through who you are in Christ. Renew your mind with the truth that your acceptance, security and significance are in Christ alone.

We recommend that you meditate on the following truths daily, perhaps reading the entire list aloud, morning and evening, for the next few weeks. Think about what you are reading and let your heart rejoice in the truth!

I renounce the lie that I am rejected, unloved, dirty or shameful because IN CHRIST I am completely accepted. God says...

> **Your acceptance, security and significance are in Christ alone.**

(Jn. 1: 12)	I am God's child.
(Jn. 15:5)	I am Jesus' chosen friend.
(Rom. 5:1)	I have been justified.
(1 Cor. 6:17)	I am united with the Lord and I am one spirit with Him.
(1 Cor. 6:19, 20)	I have been bought with a price. I belong to God.
(1 Cor. 12:27)	I am a member of Christ's body, part of His family.
(Eph. 1:1)	I am a saint, a holy one.
(Eph. 1: 5)	I have been adopted as God's child.
(Eph. 2:18)	I have direct access to God through the Holy Spirit.
(Col. 1: 14)	I have been redeemed and forgiven of all my sins.
(Col. 2: 10)	I am complete in Christ.

I renounce the lie that I am guilty, unprotected, alone or abandoned because IN CHRIST I am totally secure. God says...

> **The Scriptures are given not to increase our knowledge, but to change our lives.**
> D. L. Moody

(Rom. 8:1, 2)	I am free forever from condemnation.
(Rom. 8:28)	I am assured that all things work together for good.
(Rom. 8:31-34)	I am free from any condemning charges against me.
(Rom. 8:35-39)	I cannot be separated from the love of God.
(2 Cor. 1:21, 22)	I have been established, anointed and sealed by God.
(Phil. 1:6)	I am confident that the good work God has begun in me will be perfected.

Who I Am In Christ 95

(Phil. 3:20)	I am a citizen of heaven.
(Col. 3:3)	I am hidden with Christ in God.
(2 Tim. 1:7)	I have not been given a spirit of fear, but of power, love and a sound mind.
(Heb. 4:16)	I can find grace and mercy to help in time of need.
(1 John 5:18)	I am born of God and the evil one cannot touch me.

I renounce the lie that I am worthless, inadequate, helpless or hopeless because IN CHRIST I am deeply significant. God says...

I am not the great "I Am" but by the grace of God I am what I am.
Exodus 3:14;
John 8:24, 28, 58;
1 Corinthians 15:10

(Matt. 5:13, 14)	I am the salt of the earth and the light of the world.
(Jn. 15:1, 5)	I am a branch of the true vine, Jesus, a channel of His life.
(Jn. 15:16)	I have been chosen and appointed by God to bear fruit.
(Acts 1:8)	I am a personal, Spirit-empowered witness of Christ's.
(1 Cor. 3:16)	I am a temple where the Holy Spirit lives.
(2 Cor. 5:17-21)	I am an ambassador for Christ to bring others to Him.
(2 Cor. 6:1)	I am God's co-worker.
(Eph. 2:6)	I am seated with Christ in the heavenly realm.
(Eph. 2: 10)	I am God's workmanship, created for good works.
(Eph. 3:12)	I may approach God with freedom and confidence.
(Phil. 4:13)	I CAN DO ALL THINGS THROUGH CHRIST WHO STRENGTHENS ME!!

This ends the Freedom in Christ section. We appreciate their generosity in allowing us to use and adapt the Steps to Freedom in Christ.

96   *Who I Am In Christ*

Section Five

GO FOR THE GOALS
Workbook/Leader's Guide

Those who hope in the Lord

will soar like eagles. Isaiah 40:31

- Using Go For The Goals
- Goal One: Truth
- Goal Two: Attitude
- Goal Three: Health
- Goal Four: Decisions
- Goal Five: Faith
- Goal Six: Forgiveness

- Goal Seven: Surrender
- Goal Eight: Devotions
- Goal Nine: Fellowship
- Goal Ten: Inventory
- Goal Eleven: Victory
- Goal Twelve: Outreach
- The Overcomer's Covenant In Christ

Using Go For The Goals

In Christ, we can find daily victory in the marathon of life.

This interactive workbook helps us learn how to effectively relate to God and one another. To use "Go For The Goals" as a workbook:

- Begin by asking the Lord to give you insight.
- Make your answers personal (using "I" instead of "you").
- Find your answers in the lesson (except for questions about your feelings or personal experiences).
- Take your time and think about how to apply the lesson to yourself.
- Focus on one Goal at a time.

Group leaders: This workbook doubles as an easy-to-use leader's guide. See page 259, # 18 for how-to information.

Mentors: Using the workbook for discussion *after your disciple has done the homework* will accomplish more with less effort.

The Overcomer's Goals

Life's marathon contains hurdles we cannot ignore and win the prize. We call those hurdles the Overcomer's Goals.

(Short Form)

1. We face the truth knowing that **TRUTH** forms our lifeline to recovery.

2. We choose a positive **ATTITUDE** because attitudes lead to action.

3. We practice Christ-honoring habits one day at a time to build our **HEALTH.**

4. We find freedom to determine our destiny by making wise **DECISIONS.**

5. We put our **FAITH** in Jesus Christ who is the source of inner peace.

6. We forgive others as we experience and appreciate God's **FORGIVENESS.**

7. We **SURRENDER** our will to discover God's plan for our lives.

8. We make time for daily **DEVOTIONS** so God can transform our lives.

9. We maintain **FELLOWSHIP** with the Lord and those friends who support our recovery.

10. We keep a personal **INVENTORY** and allow the Lord to remove our defects.

11. We transfer our dependency to God to claim the **VICTORY** that is ours in Christ.

12. We gratefully **OUTREACH** by sharing the message of victory in Christ.

GOAL ONE: TRUTH

Truth forms our lifeline to recovery.

A. **WE FACE THE TRUTH KNOWING THAT TRUTH FORMS OUR LIFELINE TO RECOVERY.** We cannot run the risk of blaming our problems on God or others. Satan uses lies and false beliefs to try to enslave us. Knowing that God loves us gives us the courage to confess the truth. **"You will know the truth, and the truth will set you free."** (John 8:32)

1. How does total honesty help bring about recovery? (You may wish to refer to "What Is Christ-Centered Recovery" on page 9.)

   _____
   _____
   _____
   _____

2. How do you feel about sharing your pain with others?

   _____
   _____
   _____
   _____
   _____

3. How can painful experiences fool you into believing untruths about yourself, others, and God? (See the illustration on page 106.)

   _____
   _____
   _____
   _____
   _____

He who loses honesty has nothing else to lose.

4. In what way do lies or false beliefs enslave? Give a personal example if you can.

   _____
   _____
   _____
   _____

5. What does **"you will know the truth, and the truth will set you free"** mean to you?

_____

_____

_____

_____

_____

_____

B. Denial is deadly, so we cannot hide from our problems. *Recovery demands that we face reality regarding ourselves, our relationship with God, and our relationship with others.* Since God knows all about us, why should we deny the truth? **"Lord, You have searched me and You know me... You are familiar with all my ways." "O Lord, do not Your eyes look for truth?"** (Psalm 139:1,3; Jeremiah 5:3a)

> "Are not five sparrows sold for two pennies? Yet not one of them is forgotten by God. Indeed, the very hairs of your head are all numbered. Don't be afraid; you are worth more than many sparrows."
> Matthew 10:29-31

1. How can you be sure the Lord knows you and cares about you in spite of whatever problems you may have?

_____

_____

_____

_____

_____

_____

2. How do you feel about the fact that a loving God knows all about you?

_____

_____

_____

_____

_____

_____

> **If we live in denial, the only person we fool is ourselves.**

3. What can you do to help yourself face reality and avoid denial?

_____
_____
_____
_____
_____
_____

4. What is the truth about your relationship with family, friends, co-workers, etc.? *(Take extra time on questions four and five. Face any anger or pain you may have and express it.)*

_____
_____
_____
_____
_____
_____
_____
_____
_____
_____
_____
_____
_____
_____

5. What is the truth about your relationship with God?

> **Sin is any attempt to meet our needs independent of and apart from God.**

_____
_____
_____
_____
_____
_____

C. Truthfully, we're powerless to overcome our problems or manage our lives alone. We have absolutely no hope apart from the Lord Jesus Christ. To open the door for God's help, we admit total defeat. **"Then the woman, knowing what had happened to her, came and fell at [Jesus'] feet and... told Him the whole truth."** (Mark 5:33)

Goal One: Truth 101

1. How do you feel about admitting that you need help?

_____

2. In what way do you benefit by admitting you can do nothing apart from Jesus Christ?

_____

God allows our problems and failures to help us realize that we need Him.

3. Why is Jesus Christ your only hope for lasting victory?

_____

4. What areas in your life tend to cause you difficulty?

_____

If we think we can manage our lives on our own, God will let us.

5. What changes would you like to occur as a result of applying the *Overcomer's Handbook* to your daily life?

_____

102   *Goal One: Truth*

_____
_____
_____
_____

Defend the Bible? I would just as soon defend a lion! Just turn the Bible loose and it will defend itself.

Charles Spurgeon

D. The truth hurts, but it also heals. To recover, we replace Satan's lies with God's truth—the Bible. The Scriptures are the lifesaving remedy for the falsehood that threatens to destroy us. **"[God's] Word is truth."** No other book equals the Bible's perfect accuracy or healing power. **"All Scripture is [inspired by God] and is useful for teaching… correcting, and training in [right living], so the [person] may be [well] equipped for every good work."** (John 17:17b; 2 Timothy 3:16–17)

1. How do you know that the Bible is God's Word? (If you're not sure, refer to page 16.)

_____
_____
_____
_____
_____
_____

2. Why is it so important to apply God's Word to your own life?

_____
_____
_____
_____

3. What is God saying to you in 2 Timothy 3:16-17 above? Substitute your name for "the person" to make the Scripture personal.

_____
_____
_____
_____

The Bible is God's mind in print.

4. What likeness do you see between your childhood relationship with your parents and your idea of who God is?

_____
_____
_____

Goal One: Truth 103

_____

5. How can God's Word help you get to know Him better?

_____
_____
_____
_____
_____

Christg-centered recovery is not so much *from something* as it is *to Someone*.

E. Our own ideas only lead us into trouble. Therefore, we abandon our thoughts in favor of God's truth. **"As the heavens are higher than the earth, so are my ways higher than your ways and my thoughts than your thoughts."** We willingly listen to God's Word and seek Christ-centered recovery. Our Handbook leads us to the Lord Jesus Christ (the God of the Bible) rather than to a false god. **"Jesus answered... everyone on the side of truth listens to me."** (Isaiah 55:9; John 18:37b)

1. How do you feel about getting to know the Lord better?

_____
_____
_____
_____
_____
_____

2. What's the advantage of relying on what the Bible says rather than on your own ideas?

_____
_____
_____
_____

I can't— God can— I think I'll let Him.

3. What should you do when your opinions or feelings differ from God's truth?

_____
_____
_____

104   *Goal One: Truth*

4. Where do you see yourself in the "Where Are You" chart on page 12?

_____

_____

_____

_____

_____

Insanity: Doing the same thing over and over and expecting different results.

5. What does "If nothing changes, nothing changes." mean to you?

_____

_____

_____

_____

Evaluate Your Progress
(To be discussed with your sponsor-mentor as well as written below.)

Lasting change comes by letting the Lord work through you to accomplish each Goal. How has your life or thinking changed as a result of focusing on Goal One?

_____

_____

_____

_____

_____

_____

_____

_____

_____

_____

_____

_____

_____

"Let us throw off everything that hinders and the sin that so easily entangles us, and let us run with perseverance the race marked out for us."
Hebrews 12:1b

Goal One: Truth 105

"Train your brain" to accept truth and reject lies!

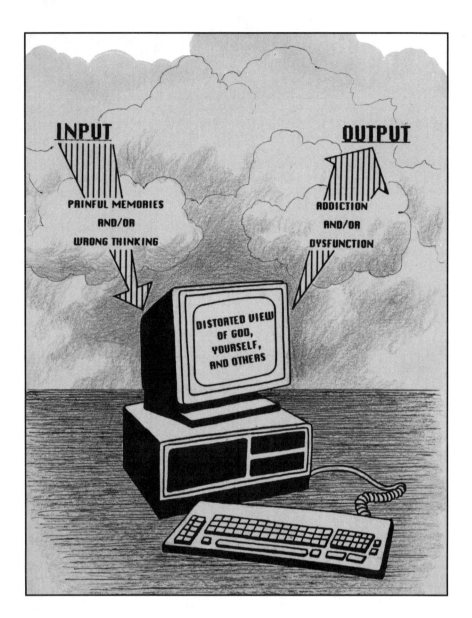

Victory is won or lost in the mind. What you choose to believe about God and yourself determines your destiny! Transform your thinking and your life by the practical application of God's Word. **"Do not conform any longer to the pattern of this world, but be transformed by the renewing of your mind."** (Romans 12:2a)

Goal Two: Attitude

Our attitude determines our altitude.

A. **We Choose a Positive Attitude Because Attitudes Lead to Action.** As we appreciate daily blessings, we develop a thankful attitude. We're grateful that through Jesus Christ we have hope. Jesus said, **"In this world you will have trouble. But take heart! I have overcome the world."** When we look at things from God's perspective, we overcome life's problems. **"This is the victory that has overcome the world, even our faith."** (John 16:33; 1 John 5:4)

1. What's the big deal about attitude?

2. How does looking at life from God's viewpoint improve your attitude?

3. How can God's Word help you gain His perspective on life?

I am convinced that life is 10% what happens to me and 90% how I react to it. And so it is with you. We are in charge of our attitudes.
Charles Swindoll

Goal Two: Attitude

4. What are some ways your attitude affects the people closest to you?

_____
_____
_____
_____
_____
_____

You can live on Grumble St. or Thanksgiving Ave.

5. How does realizing that attitude is a choice help you grow?

_____
_____
_____
_____
_____
_____

B. A good attitude lifts us above the storms of life. Attitude comes from our feelings and thoughts. By choosing what to think about, we change our feelings. Thinking about what is true, good, and right leads us into recovery. **"Fix your thoughts on what is true and good and right. Think about things that are pure and lovely, and dwell on the fine, good things in others. Think about all you can praise God for and be glad about."** (Philippians 4:8 LB)

1. How does what you think about affect how you feel?

_____
_____
_____
_____

By choosing what to think about, we can change our feelings.

2. What happens if you allow your feelings to control your behavior?

_____
_____
_____
_____

108 *Goal Two: Attitude*

> **The past makes a valuable guidepost but a dangerous hitching post.**

3. How can you deal with painful memories and feelings and yet keep a positive attitude about life?

_____

4. How does sharing your pain with those you trust help you let it go?

_____

> **"A heart at peace gives life to the body, but envy rots the bones."**
> Proverbs 14:30

5. How does your attitude affect your health?

_____

C. **"As [a person] thinks in his heart, so is he."** Our thoughts lay down the tracks on which our life train runs. Therefore, we take responsibility for our thought life. We experience victory as we reject false beliefs and accept the truth. (Proverbs 23:7 NKJV)

   To live a new life, we change our habits;
   To change our habits, we change our choices;
   To change our choices, we change our thinking;
   To change our thinking, we believe God's truth.

Goal Two: Attitude 109

> Be careful what you put in your mind. Garbage in— garbage out.

1. What does **"As a person thinks in his heart, so is he."** mean to you?

_____

_____

_____

_____

_____

_____

2. How does what you read affect your thinking? (Give an example.)

_____

_____

_____

_____

_____

3. How does what you watch or listen to change how you think? (Give an example.)

_____

_____

_____

_____

_____

_____

4. In what ways do the people you spend your time with influence your thinking?

_____

_____

_____

_____

_____

_____

> When clouds of depression hang low, praise will drive them away.
> Don Gossett

5. How can you change your thinking?

_____

_____

110 *Goal Two: Attitude*

> Minds are like parachutes. The only time they function is when they're open.

D. We keep an open mind. An open mind welcomes the truth while a closed mind resists. Change may be frightening but not nearly so frightening as the consequences of refusing to change. Once we built our life on the sand of our own misbeliefs. Now we build on the solid rock of God's truth. Jesus said, **"Everyone who hears these words of mine and puts them into practice is like a wise man who built his house on the rock. The rain came down, the streams rose, and the winds blew and beat against that house; yet it did not fall because it had its foundation on the rock. But everyone who hears these words of mine and does not put them into practice is like a foolish man who built his house on sand. The rain came down, the streams rose, and the winds blew and beat against that house, and it fell with a great crash."** (Matthew 7:24–27)

1. In what way does recovery require an open mind?

2. How can you overcome the fear of change?

3. What happens if you base your actions on false beliefs?

> To find God's treasure house of blessing, climb the ladder of His divine promises.

Goal Two: Attitude 111

4. How can you build your life on the rock of God's truth?

_____

_____

_____

_____

_____

_____

5. How might Satan try to keep you from building on the rock?

_____

_____

_____

_____

_____

_____

_____

Be humble or you'll stumble.
D.L. Moody

E. **"Pride goes before destruction and a [cocky attitude] before a fall." "So if you think you are standing firm, be careful that you don't fall."** Even though we take steps toward recovery, we will stumble if we become overconfident. Pride is a high-wire on which we dare not walk. **"Everyone who exalts himself will be [brought low], but he who humbles himself will be [lifted up]."** (Proverbs 16:18; 1 Corinthians 10:12; Luke 18:14)

1. What are the dangers of becoming proud?

_____

_____

_____

_____

_____

_____

Humility is putting no confidence in ourselves, but rather in the Lord.

2. How does pride differ from a healthy feeling of self-worth? (See the definition of healthy self-esteem on page 203.)

_____

_____

_____

112　*Goal Two: Attitude*

Are you a human being or a "human doing"? What you are determines what you do and not the other way around.

3. What do you base your sense of self-worth on?

4. In what way does self-respect require doing what you know God would have you do?

5. What does it mean to humble yourself?

The way up with God is down!

Goal Two continues on the following page...

Goal Two: Attitude 113

Evaluate Your Progress

(To be discussed with your sponsor-mentor as well as written below.)

Lasting change comes by letting the Lord work through you to accomplish each Goal. How has your life or thinking changed as a result of focusing on Goal Two?

_____

_____

_____

_____

_____

_____

_____

_____

_____

_____

_____

_____

_____

"Let us throw off everything that hinders and the sin that so easily entangles us, and let us run with perseverance the race marked out for us."

Hebrews 12:1b

Notes

114   *Goal Two: Attitude*

Goal Three: Health

Giving in to sinful behavior is like grabbing a tiger by the tail!

A. **WE PRACTICE CHRIST-HONORING HABITS ONE DAY AT A TIME TO BUILD OUR HEALTH.** Giving in to sinful behavior would be like grabbing a tiger by the tail! Instead, we put our energies into wholesome activities. We've found that every area of health affects our whole person. **"A cheerful heart is good medicine, but a crushed spirit dries up the bones." "May your whole spirit, soul, and body be [preserved until] the coming of our Lord Jesus Christ."** (Proverbs 17:22; 1 Thessalonians 5:23b)

1. Why is your health such a vital part of your recovery?

   _____
   _____
   _____
   _____
   _____
   _____
   _____
   _____

2. What will happen if you stop bad habits but do not replace them with wholesome ones?

   _____
   _____
   _____
   _____
   _____

3. How does substituting one unhealthy behavior for another prevent recovery? (See cross-addiction definition on page 202.)

   _____
   _____
   _____
   _____
   _____

If you don't take care of your health, where will you live when your body wears out?

4. How does taking one day at a time make recovery easier?

   _____
   _____

Goal Three: Health 115

He who laughs lasts.

5. How does a cheerful heart affect your health?

_____

_____

_____

_____

_____

_____

_____

B. Knowing that God cares about us, we care about ourselves. **"Are not five sparrows sold for two pennies? Yet not one of them is forgotten by God. Indeed, the very hairs of your head are all numbered. Don't be afraid; you are worth more than many sparrows."** Caring about ourselves includes adequate rest, proper nutrition, exercise, and stress management. We do what we can to build our health, and trust God for the results. (Luke 12:6–7)

1. How does knowing God cares about you affect how you treat your body?

_____

_____

_____

_____

_____

_____

We cannot ignore health issues and fulfill the purpose for which God made us.

2. In what ways do you need to take better care of your body?

_____

_____

_____

_____

_____

_____

116   _Goal Three: Health_

3. How does getting enough sleep affect other areas of your life?

If we would take better care of our health, we could put prayer emphasis on spiritual matters rather than physical.

4. What do exercise and physical fitness have to do with recovery?

5. What can you do to overcome the pressures of life? (Refer to stress management on page 203.)

C. We want to feel well, so we educate ourselves about good nutrition. Healthful snacks instead of coffee, sweets, and cigarettes help avoid artificial highs and cravings. Nutritious snacks include nuts, lowfat cheeses, whole grain crackers, fresh fruits, and vegetables. We also drink at least eight glasses of pure water every day. **"Whether you eat or drink, or whatever you do, do it all for the glory of God"**—and your own good. (1 Corinthians 10:31)

Do you live to eat or eat to live?

1. How do you know God cares about what you eat and drink?

Goal Three: Health 117

> "Do you not know that your body is a temple of the Holy Spirit, who is in you, whom you have received from God?"
> 1 Corinthians 6:19

2. What are some reasons to be concerned about good nutrition?

_____

_____

_____

_____

_____

3. How do caffeine, sugar, and cigarettes affect your recovery?

_____

_____

_____

_____

_____

4. What are some nutritious snacks you can substitute for junk foods?

_____

_____

_____

_____

_____

> "Everything is permissible for me— but not everything is beneficial."
> 1 Corinthians 6:12

5. What specific change will you make this week to improve your health?

_____

_____

_____

_____

_____

D. We take personal responsibility for decisions about our health. We choose a doctor who promotes preventive health care and avoids prescribing drugs whenever possible. As we educate ourselves about health care, we lean on the Lord for wisdom. He can use any means He chooses to heal us whether slowly or quickly. We avoid the mistake of expecting doctors to do what only God can do. **"Even in his illness he did not seek help from the Lord, but only from the physicians."** (2 Chronicles 16:12b)

118   *Goal Three: Health*

A healthy mind and body does not crave drugs or alcohol.

1. What can you do to learn more about preventive health care? (We recommend *What the Bible says About Healthy Living* by Rex Russell,M.D., published by Regal Books.)

_____

_____

_____

_____

_____

2. How can you depend on the Lord and seek professional help at the same time?

_____

_____

_____

_____

_____

3. What can you do when a doctor is unavailable or unable to help?

_____

_____

_____

_____

4. Why can addictive prescription drugs be harmful? (Refer to the definition of cross-addiction on page 202.)

_____

_____

_____

_____

_____

Bringing the Lord Jesus into every aspect of life will improve your health. He is the Great Physician!

5. In what way is your health in your hands while at the same time being in God's hand?

_____

_____

_____

_____

_____

Goal Three: Health 119

E. God made each of us a one-of-a-kind "Designer original." Because we are precious to our Maker, we do not damage or destroy our bodies. **"For You created my inmost being; You knit me together in my mother's womb. I praise You for I am fearfully and wonderfully made; Your works are wonderful, I know that full well... All the days [of my life] were written in Your book before one of them came to be. How precious it is, Lord, to realize that You are thinking about me constantly."** (Psalm 139:13–17—last verse LB)

1. In what way does it make you feel special to know that God formed you in your mother's womb?

_____

_____

_____

_____

_____

_____

You are God's masterpiece.

2. What does **"I am fearfully and wonderfully made"** mean to you?

_____

_____

_____

_____

_____

3. How does knowing that God thinks about you constantly make you feel?

_____

_____

_____

_____

_____

The Lord says, "I have loved you with an everlasting love... I will build you up again."
Jeremiah 31:3-4a

120   *Goal Three: Health*

4. How does knowing you are special to God affect your feelings toward Him?

_____

_____

_____

_____

_____

_____

Giving your expectations to God takes the pressure off your relationship with others.

5. In what way does knowing you are special to God help you relate better to others?

_____

_____

_____

_____

_____

Evaluate Your Progress
(To be discussed with your sponsor-mentor as well as written below.)

Lasting change comes by letting the Lord work through you to accomplish each Goal. How has your life or thinking changed as a result of focusing on Goal Three?

_____

_____

_____

_____

_____

_____

_____

_____

_____

_____

_____

_____

"Let us throw off everything that hinders and the sin that so easily entangles us, and let us run with perseverance the race marked out for us."
Hebrews 12:1b

Go For The Goals
Workbook/Leader's Guide

Goal Three: Health 121

Notes

Good health is a
gift from God
that comes as
we treat our
bodies properly.

GOAL FOUR: DECISIONS

Our decisions determine our destiny.

A. **WE FIND FREEDOM TO DETERMINE OUR DESTINY BY MAKING WISE DECISIONS.** We realize that every choice we make causes either positive or negative results. While we cannot change our past, we can make good choices concerning our future. The most important decision we make is to put God first in everything we do. If we fail to decide, we decide to fail. To neglect Christ would be to reject Him. **"But seek first [God's] kingdom and His righteousness, and [other things you need] will be given to you as well."** (Matthew 6:33)

1. How can realizing you have choices change your life?

   _____
   _____
   _____
   _____
   _____

2. How would putting God first affect your decisions?

   _____
   _____
   _____
   _____
   _____

3. In what way do others influence your decisions?

   _____
   _____
   _____
   _____

4. How can you determine whether a decision is wise?

   _____
   _____
   _____
   _____
   _____

Wise decisions follow the principles in God's Word, (our "how-to" manual for life).

Goal Four: Decisions

5. What does "If we fail to decide, we decide to fail." mean to you?

_____

_____

_____

_____

_____

Decisions have to do not only with choosing good over evil but with choosing the best from the good.

B. God never forces us to love Him. The decision to seek Him is our personal choice and responsibility. God pleads with us not to destroy ourselves but to come to Him with our problems. **"I have set before you life and death, blessings and curses. Now choose life so that you and your children may live… for the Lord is your life."** We know that to reach God, we must come through His Son, Jesus Christ. Jesus said, **"I am the way and the truth and the life. No one comes to the Father except through me."** (Deuteronomy 30:19b–20; John 14:6)

1. Why do you think God gives you the freedom to seek or neglect Him?

_____

_____

_____

_____

_____

_____

2. Why does God allow you to feel the consequences of wrong choices?

_____

_____

_____

_____

_____

Sow a thought reap an action; sow an action reap a habit; sow a habit reap a destiny.

3. What does it mean to seek God?

_____

_____

_____

_____

_____

_____

124 *Goal Four: Decisions*

4. For what reasons should you seek God regardless of what others may think?

_____

_____

_____

_____

_____

Your answer to this question determines your destiny in this life and eternity.

5. Who is Jesus Christ to you?

_____

_____

_____

_____

_____

C. Along with all mankind, we have sinned. **"All have sinned and fallen short of the glory of God."** We're grateful that God loves us even though He hates the wrong that we do. When we admit our need, Jesus tenderly invites us to come to Him. **"I have not come to call the righteous but sinners to repentance." "Come to me all you who are weary and burdened, and I will give you rest."** (Romans 3:23; Luke 5:32; Matthew 11:28)

1. How do you feel about admitting your sin?

_____

_____

_____

_____

Our needs become blessings if they cause us to seek the Lord.

2. Why does Jesus invite you to come to Him?

_____

_____

_____

_____

3. How will coming to the Lord affect you in this life and the life to come?

_____

_____

_____

Goal Four: Decisions 125

> Grace is God's
> undeserved favor.
> Without it we'd
> all be in trouble.

4. How does knowing that God loves you in spite of your sin affect your relationship with Him?

_____

_____

_____

_____

_____

5. How does realizing that God loves people but hates their sin affect your attitude toward others?

_____

_____

_____

_____

_____

D. **"*Now* is the time of God's favor, *now* is the day of salvation." "Do not boast about tomorrow for you do not know what a day may bring forth."** We don't know all that our future holds, but we do know Who holds the future. In the Lord Jesus Christ, we find our security and our destiny. Therefore, we make our relationship with Him our top priority. (2 Corinthians 6:2; Proverbs 27:1)

1. Why is time one of your most valuable resources?

_____

> Time is the stuff
> life is made of.
> Don't waste it.

_____

_____

_____

_____

2. How can indecision waste your time and your life?

_____

_____

_____

_____

126   *Goal Four: Decisions*

3. What are the dangers of waiting until later to make time for the Lord?

_____

_____

_____

_____

4. What are some ways Satan tries to prevent you from dealing with spiritual matters?

Obedience to God's will today means that He assumes the responsibility for our tomorrow.
Charles L. Allen

_____

_____

_____

_____

_____

_____

5. How does the uncertainty of the future affect your attitude toward the Lord?

_____

_____

_____

_____

E. Pretending gets us nowhere. So after making a decision, we act on it with our whole heart. We turn our thoughts and energy toward the Lord and away from distractions. We don't allow anyone or anything to hold us back—not even our own tendency to avoid reality. The Lord says, **"You will seek me and find me when you search for me with all your heart."** (Jeremiah 29:13 NKJV)

1. How can you tell if you are seeking the Lord with your whole heart?

You can tell where your heart is by where you put your time and energy.

_____

_____

_____

_____

_____

_____

_____

_____

_____

Goal Four: Decisions 127

2. How does whether you take action on a decision reveal whether you are wholehearted?

_____

_____

_____

_____

_____

> "The one who comes to me I will by no means cast out."
> John 6:37b NKJV

3. What is God's response when you seek Him with all your heart?

_____

_____

_____

_____

4. What are some of the distractions that tend to keep you away from God's best for you?

_____

_____

_____

_____

_____

_____

> Christ is our strength, our motivation, and our life; without Him, we're going nowhere.

5. In what ways are you making room for God in your life?

_____

_____

_____

_____

_____

_____

_____

_____

Evaluate Your Progress
(To be discussed with your sponsor-mentor as well as written below.)

Lasting change comes by letting the Lord work through you to accomplish each Goal. How has your life or thinking changed as a result of focusing on Goal Four?

_____

_____

_____

_____

_____

_____

_____

_____

_____

_____

_____

_____

_____

_____

"Let us throw off everything that hinders and the sin that so easily entangles us, and let us run with perseverance the race marked out for us."
Hebrews 12:1b

Notes

Goal Four: Decisions 129

Notes

> Straight
> living cannot
> come out of
> crooked thinking.
> John Baker

GOAL FIVE: FAITH

The cross allows us to come near to God.

Faith causes the believer to hold right values and therefore, to make wise decisions.
Charles Stanley

A. **WE PUT OUR FAITH IN JESUS CHRIST WHO IS THE SOURCE OF INNER PEACE.** Fear is the absence of faith. Because God loves us and won't deceive us, we come to Him in faith. **"God is not a man, that He should lie, nor a son of man, that He should change His mind. Does He speak and then not act? Does He promise and not fulfill?"** Jesus said, **"Whoever comes to me I will never drive away."** (Numbers 23:19; John 6:37)

1. Why is faith in Jesus Christ the only way you can find true inner peace?

   _____
   _____
   _____
   _____
   _____

2. What difference does it make whether you are controlled by fear or faith?

   _____
   _____
   _____
   _____

3. In your own words, what is faith?

   _____
   _____
   _____
   _____

4. How can you be sure God will never deceive you or let you down as others may have done?

   _____
   _____
   _____

Goal Five: Faith   131

_____

_____

_____

5. How does knowing that Jesus is always there for you affect your attitude toward Him?

_____

_____

_____

_____

_____

_____

Little faith will bring your soul to heaven. Great faith will bring heaven to your soul.
Charles Spurgeon

(The remainder of this Goal substitutes "I" and "me" for "we" and "us.")

B. Peace with God doesn't depend on religion or good works but on accepting God's gift of eternal life. **"For by grace you have been saved through faith—and this not from yourselves, it is the gift of God—not by works so that no one can boast."** By faith I let Jesus take my sins and problems. In exchange, He gives me eternal life and peace. **"For the wages of sin is death, but the gift of God is eternal life through Jesus Christ our Lord."** (Ephesians 2:8–9; Romans 6:23 KJV)

1. How can you make eternal life and inner peace yours?

_____

_____

_____

_____

2. What will happen if you try to *earn* God's love and eternal life?

_____

_____

_____

_____

Fear is simply unbelief in disguise.

3. How can fear hold you back from accepting eternal life and all the good things that God has for His children?

_____

_____

_____

132 *Goal Five: Faith*

_____
_____
_____
_____

Fear overcomes us only when we feel distant from God.

4. In what way can self-will keep you from accepting God's gift?

_____
_____
_____
_____
_____

5. Are you enjoying God's gift of eternal life? Why or why not?

_____
_____
_____
_____
_____

C. Knowing that Jesus died for others is not enough to make me an overcomer. Instead, I accept Christ as my personal Savior and the Source of my new life. **"For God so loved the world that He gave His one and only Son, that whoever believes in Him shall not perish but have eternal life."** God says that by trusting in His Son, I *have* eternal life. To think that I get eternal life, and all that goes with it, just by taking God at His Word! (John 3:16)

1. Make John 3:16 personal, by putting in your name. Then tell what each part of the verse means to you.

The world says that "seeing is believing," but God wants us to believe in order to see.

- **"For God so loved** _____
  your name

  _____
  _____

- **that He gave His one and only Son,**

  _____
  _____

Goal Five: Faith 133

- **that** _____ **who believes in Him**

  your name

  _____

  _____

- **shall not perish**

  _____

  _____

- **but have eternal life."**

  _____

  _____

To overcome, spend much time thinking about God's promises and little time thinking about your problems.

2. How has God demonstrated His love to you?

   _____

   _____

   _____

   _____

   _____

3. How can you get eternal life and all that goes with it?

   _____

   _____

   _____

   _____

4. What does it mean to believe God?

   _____

   _____

   _____

   _____

5. What are some of the ways Satan tries to make you doubt God's Word?

   _____

   _____

134 *Goal Five: Faith*

> **Faith honors God and God honors faith.**
> Thomas Champness

D. Faith is the hand that takes what God offers. **"Faith comes from hearing [God's] message."** Instead of looking within to see how little faith I have, I simply take God at His Word. My new life is based on what He says, not on my feelings or behavior. I make God's Word personal by reading it thoughtfully and applying it to myself. I know that God follows through on His promises because **"it is impossible for God to lie."** (Romans 10:17a; Hebrews 6:18b)

1. What will happen if you simply know about the Lord but do not really depend on Him?

2. Why should you rely on what God says instead of your feelings?

> **Are you a "fair-weather Christian" who only praises the Lord when things go well?**

3. Whenever you refuse to believe God, what are you suggesting about Him?

4. How can you get more faith?

Goal Five: Faith 135

_____

_____

Even the devil quoted God's Word. He doesn't care if you read the Bible as long as you don't apply it to your life.

5. Which of the following pitfalls is a problem for you, and how will you overcome it?

- Keeping too busy to read God's Word
- Trying to earn your new life rather than accept it by faith
- Failing to realize that God won't let you down even though others have
- Focusing on your feelings instead of God's Word
- Reading God's Word so rapidly that you don't realize what He is saying
- Applying God's Word to everyone else instead of yourself

_____

_____

_____

_____

_____

_____

E. By accepting Jesus Christ as my Savior, I become God's child. Christ's death paid for my sins, and His rising from the dead gives me new life. **"To [all] who received Him [by believing] in His name, He gave the right to become children of God."** By faith I claim my new identity so my life will change. For **"we live by faith, not by sight."** (John 1:12; 2 Corinthians 5:7)

1. Briefly, how and when did you become God's child?

_____

_____

_____

_____

_____

Fear releases the destructive power of Satan; faith releases the creative power of God.

2. What are some of the things God gives His children in addition to a home in heaven?

_____

_____

_____

136 *Goal Five: Faith*

> Praise is the language of faith.
> Don Gossett

3. How does realizing you are God's child affect your daily life?

4. How can you avoid letting circumstances disturb your peace with the Lord?

> Fear and faith cannot exist together. When one enters, the other departs.

5. What does **"We live by faith, not by sight."** mean to you?

Goal Five: Faith 137

Evaluate Your Progress
(To be discussed with your sponsor-mentor as well as written below.)

Lasting change comes by letting the Lord work through you to accomplish each Goal. How has your life or thinking changed as a result of focusing on Goal Five?

_____
_____
_____
_____
_____
_____
_____
_____
_____
_____
_____
_____
_____
_____

"Let us throw off everything that hinders and the sin that so easily entangles us, and let us run with perseverance the race marked out for us."
Hebrews 12:1b

Notes

138   *Goal Five: Faith*

Goal Six: Forgiveness

Forgiveness begins and ends at the cross.

A. **We Forgive Others as We Experience and Appreciate God's Forgiveness.** To make forgiveness ours, we accept it by faith. Accepting Christ's death for us makes forgiving others easier. Whenever we struggle with guilt or resentment, we focus on the cross. Since Christ gave Himself for our sins, how can we refuse to forgive others? **"Shouldn't you have mercy on your fellow [man] just as I had on you?" "Forgive as the Lord forgave you."** (Matthew 18:33; Colossians 3:13b)

1. What does God's forgiveness mean to you?

   _____
   _____
   _____
   _____
   _____
   _____

2. How can you experience God's forgiveness?

   _____
   _____
   _____
   _____

3. What will result if you refuse to accept God's forgiveness?

   _____
   _____
   _____
   _____

4. How is accepting God's forgiveness the key to forgiving yourself?

   _____
   _____
   _____
   _____
   _____
   _____

The shed blood of Christ allows us to give and receive forgiveness.

5. How does appreciating God's forgiveness make it easier to forgive others?

_____

_____

_____

_____

_____

_____

_____

(The remainder of this Goal substitutes "I" and "me" for "we" and "us.")

"They overcame by the blood of the Lamb."
Revelation 12:11

B. No matter how low I sink, I never get to the bottom of God's love. **"God demonstrates His own love for us in this: while we were still sinners, Christ died for us."** It doesn't take any more or less of Jesus' blood to cleanse me than anyone else. Knowing this gives me peace and keeps me from having a faultfinding attitude. **"I tell you... there will be more rejoicing in heaven over one sinner who [has a change of heart] than over ninety-nine righteous persons who do not need to repent."** (Romans 5:8; Luke 15:7)

1. How can refusing to admit your sin prevent you from giving or receiving forgiveness?

_____

_____

_____

_____

_____

_____

_____

If I point a finger at you, I have three pointing back at myself.

2. Can anyone's sins be so awful that they are greater than the power of Christ's cleansing blood? Explain.

_____

_____

_____

_____

_____

_____

_____

140   *Goal Six: Forgiveness*

3. In what way can the shed blood of Christ help you avoid a fault-finding attitude?

_____

_____

_____

_____

_____

_____

When you refuse to forgive others, you allow them to continue hurting you.

4. What are some consequences of refusing to forgive those who have wronged you?

_____

_____

_____

_____

_____

_____

_____

5. How can denying the pain others have caused prevent you from truly forgiving them?

_____

_____

_____

_____

_____

When I realize the awful price God paid for my sin, how can I look down on anyone else?

C. What a sight to picture the innocent Son of God bleeding and dying for my sins! **"He himself bore [my] sins in His body on the [cross]."** Because Jesus took my punishment, God has given me a full pardon and new life. Jesus rose from the dead proving that God is satisfied with His payment for *all* my sins—past, present, and future. I know that my sins don't need to be paid for twice. **"Christ died for sins once for all, the [holy] for the [unholy], to bring [me] to God."** (1 Peter 2:24; 3:18)

1. What makes you acceptable to God and removes your guilt?

_____

_____

_____

Goal Six: Forgiveness 141

> "If righteousness could be gained through [good works], Christ died for nothing."
> Galatians 2:21b

_____

2. What happens if you try to earn God's forgiveness instead of accepting His unconditional love as a gift?

_____

_____

_____

_____

3. If you died and God asked you why He should let you into Heaven, what would you tell Him?

_____

_____

_____

_____

4. How do you know for sure that Christ died for *all* your sins?

_____

_____

_____

_____

> "...we have One who has been tempted in every way, just as we are—yet was without sin. Let us then approach [His throne] with confidence, so that we may find help in our time of need."
> Hebrews 4:14-16

5. What are some of the benefits of having a living Savior in heaven?

_____

_____

_____

_____

D. I leave my past behind by accepting God's truth instead of my misbeliefs. Jesus said, **"I tell you the truth, whoever hears my Word and believes Him who sent me has eternal life and will not be condemned; he has crossed over from death to life."** Jesus' promise assures me that I'm not condemned. It amazes me to think that **"as far as the east is from the west, so far has [God] removed [my] sins from [me]."** (John 5:24; Psalm 103:12)

142   *Goal Six: Forgiveness*

1. Make John 5:24 personal by putting in your name. Then tell what each part of the verse means to you.

- **"I tell you the truth**

  _____

  _____

- _____ **who hears my Word**

your name

  _____

  _____

- **and believes Him who sent me**

  _____

  _____

- **has eternal life**

  _____

  _____

- **and will not be condemned;**

  _____

  _____

- _____ **has crossed over from death to life."**

your name

  _____

  _____

2. How does it make you feel to know that you are not condemned?

  _____

  _____

  _____

  _____

  _____

Make the Word of God personal to get its benefit.

You can never break God's promises by leaning on them.

GO FOR THE GOALS
Workbook/Leader's Guide

Goal Six: Forgiveness 143

3. Does leaving your past behind mean that you should expect to live perfectly? Explain.

> "If we claim to be without sin, we deceive ourselves and the truth is not in us."
> 1 John 1:8

4. What from your past are you most relieved about leaving behind?

5. How can you thank God for giving you eternal life?

> Christ gave His life for us to give His life to us and live His life through us.

144   *Goal Six: Forgiveness*

> "If what he has built survives, he will receive his reward. If it is burned up, he will suffer loss; he himself will be saved, but only as one escaping through the flames."
> 1 Corinthians 3:11-15

E. Once I accept God's forgiveness, I'm guaranteed new life and a home in heaven. Jesus said, **"I give to them eternal life, and they shall never perish; no one can snatch them out of my hand. My Father, who has given them to me, is greater than all; no one can snatch them out of my Father's hand."** Since God's Word never changes, I will always be His child. Knowing I'm secure in God's love allows me to forgive those who have wronged me. **"For Christ's love [motivates me]."** (John 10:28–29; 2 Corinthians 5:14a)

1. If you've been born into God's family, how can you be sure eternal life will always be yours?

_____

_____

_____

_____

_____

_____

2. Because God has forgiven all your sins, what should you do to those who've wronged you?

_____

_____

_____

_____

_____

_____

3. What are some of the benefits of forgiving others?

> "When a [person's] ways please the Lord, He makes even his enemies to be at peace with him."
> Proverbs 16:7 NKJV

_____

_____

_____

_____

_____

_____

_____

_____

Goal Six: Forgiveness

4. If you haven't already done so, go through the Steps to Freedom on pages 45 to 96. If possible, find an experienced encourager to help you. (If you have already gone through the Steps to Freedom, how did doing so impact your life?)

Do not let the sun go down while you are still angry and do not give the devil a foothold.
Ephesians 4:26-27

_____

_____

_____

_____

_____

_____

_____

5. If anger continues to come up toward someone who has offended you, think again about what *your* sin did to the Lord Jesus! Then repeat the Step to Freedom, "Bitterness vs. Forgiveness" on pages 69-73.

Evaluate Your Progress
(To be discussed with your sponsor-mentor as well as written below.)

Lasting change comes by letting the Lord work through you to accomplish each Goal. How has your life or thinking changed as a result of focusing on Goal Six?

_____

_____

_____

_____

_____

_____

_____

_____

_____

_____

"Let us throw off everything that hinders and the sin that so easily entangles us, and let us run with perseverance the race marked out for us."
Hebrews 12:1b

146   *Goal Six: Forgiveness*

Goal Seven: Surrender

How can we help but surrender to His love?

A. **We Surrender Our Will to Discover God's Plan for Our Lives.** "**For I know the plans I have for you, declares the Lord, plans to prosper you and not to harm you, plans to give you hope and a future.**" Trusting God enough to surrender every day and every issue to Him makes us overcomers. Even in difficulties we find inner joy as we give Jesus full control. "**Not my will but Yours be done**" is our constant prayer. (Jeremiah 29:11; Luke 22:42b)

1. What does it mean to surrender to God?

2. How does surrender help you discover God's plan for your life?

3. In what way does what you believe about God affect your willingness to surrender to Him?

Some of us live as though our plan for our lives is better than God's.

4. How does knowing Christ as a living, loving Savior make it easier to trust Him with your future?

Goal Seven: Surrender 147

> Before we can pray, "Thy kingdom come," we must be willing to pray, "My kingdom go".
> Alan Redpath

5. Why is surrender daily rather than once and for all?

B. Once we've accepted Christ, we have a new Master living within. Yielding to Him releases us from sin's awful power. **"Thank God, though you were once slaves [to] sin, you have become obedient with all your heart to the teaching [by] which you were instructed… And having been set free from sin, you have become servants of [what is right]."** Yielding requires heartfelt obedience to our loving Lord. Surrendering to Him helps us win the battle against sin and Satan. **"If the Son sets you free, you will be free indeed."** (Romans 6:17–18 Amplified Bible; John 8:36)

1. What does **"If the Son sets you free, you will be free indeed."** mean to you?

> Freedom means freedom to live for the Lord not freedom to do whatever we please.

2. What does it mean to yield to your new Master, and what if you don't feel like it?

3. How does obedience to the Lord help you overcome sin and Satan?

148   *Goal Seven: Surrender*

_____

A lack of contentment indicates a need to surrender.

4. What are some consequences of allowing your old self to regain control?

_____

5. What tends to hold you back from total surrender?

_____

C. Self-obsession has been the root of our problems. *We find recovery and fulfillment by centering our world around Christ instead of ourselves.* **"He died for all [so] that those who live should no longer live for themselves but for Him who died for them and was raised again."** How can we help but love the Lord, and let Him have control, when He shed His blood for us? **"How great is the love the Father has [poured out] on us."** (2 Corinthians 5:15; 1 John 3:1a)

A relationship with God is more, but not less, than any other relationship.

1. How can focusing on the Lord's unconditional love make you more willing to surrender to Him?

_____

2. What does it mean to center your life around Christ?

_____

Goal Seven: Surrender 149

> Don't bother to give God instructions, just report for duty.
>
> Corrie ten Boom

3. Describe the differences between a self-centered and a Christ-centered life.

_____

_____

_____

_____

_____

4. How can you develop a more Christ-centered life?

_____

_____

_____

_____

_____

_____

> It doesn't take a great man to be a great Christian; it just takes all there is of him.
>
> Seth Wilson

5. What specific area of your life are you turning over to the Lord today?

_____

_____

_____

_____

_____

D. It's impossible to do the Lord's will in our own strength. Instead of struggling to live the "Christian life," *we allow Christ to live through us.* When making decisions about what we do, where we go, or what we watch, we ask ourselves, "What would Jesus do?" We surrender the right to control our lives or the lives of others. **"I have been crucified with Christ, and I no longer live, but Christ lives in me. The life I live in the body, I live by faith in the Son of God who loved me and gave Himself for me."** (Galatians 2:20)

1. What are some reasons to allow Christ to live through you instead of struggling to live the "Christian life"?

2. Why does surrender to the Lord need to be unconditional?

A dead person does not respond to temptation.

3. How does recognizing that your old self is dead help you change?

4. How does getting rid of books, music, paraphernalia, etc. relating to your old self help your spiritual growth?

The person who lacks self-control will invariably try to control others.

5. How can you avoid trying to control the lives of others?

Goal Seven: Surrender 151

> **When we get excited about a game, the world calls us a fan. When we get excited about our God, they call us a fanatic.**

E. If Christ is worth anything, He's worth everything. **"One thing I do, forgetting what is behind and straining toward what is ahead, I press on toward the goal to win the prize for which God has called me..."** As we follow God's will with our whole heart, life takes on new meaning. Putting the Lord in control gives us purpose and direction. Jesus said, **"I have come that they might have life and have it to the full."** (Philippians 3:13b–14; John 10:10)

1. In what ways does surrender to the Lord give you purpose and direction?

2. How has surrendering to the Lord changed what you hope to achieve in life?

> **Even if you're on the right track, you'll get run over if you just sit there.**
> Will Rogers

3. What are the benefits of focusing on Christ-centered goals rather than on the past?

152 *Goal Seven: Surrender*

> **"If you obey my [Word] you will remain in my love... so that my joy may be in you and your joy may be complete."**
> John 15:9-11

4. Some people think that surrendering to the Lord takes all the fun out of life. How can you prove this is one of Satan's lies?

_____
_____
_____
_____
_____
_____

5. In what ways has surrendering to the Lord has brought you joy?

_____
_____
_____
_____
_____

Evaluate Your Progress
(To be discussed with your sponsor-mentor as well as written below.)

Lasting change comes by letting the Lord work through you to accomplish each Goal. How has your life or thinking changed as a result of focusing on Goal Seven?

_____
_____
_____
_____
_____
_____
_____
_____
_____
_____
_____

> **"Let us throw off everything that hinders and the sin that so easily entangles us, and let us run with perseverance the race marked out for us."**
> Hebrews 12:1b

Goal Seven: Surrender 153

Notes

Joy is not so much getting what you want as wanting what you get.

154   *Goal Seven: Surrender*

GOAL EIGHT: DEVOTIONS

We treasure God's Word more than our daily food.

"We love because He first loved us."
1 John 4:19

A. **WE MAKE TIME FOR DAILY DEVOTIONS SO GOD CAN TRANSFORM OUR LIVES.** Devotions involve getting to know God by spending time in His Word and prayer. **"Draw near to God and He will draw near to you."** When we really know God, we discover love we never knew existed. **"God is love,"** and He fills the vacuum in our hearts. Meaningful devotions help keep our thinking straight, our lives clean, and our souls satisfied. Neglecting our quiet time with the Lord would stop our spiritual growth and rob us of our joy. (James 4:8; 1 John 4:16b)

1. How can you fill the vacuum that's left when you give up sinful behavior?

   _____
   _____
   _____
   _____
   _____

2. What does the term "daily devotions" mean to you?

   _____
   _____
   _____
   _____

3. Why are devotions essential to your new life?

   _____
   _____
   _____
   _____

4. When you draw near to God, how do you know that He will be there for you?

   _____
   _____
   _____
   _____

Goal Eight: Devotions 155

5. What Bible verse have you recently enjoyed, and what did you get out of it? (If you're not yet having devotions, the best way to get started is to get started. Set aside at least 15 minutes every day. Spend part of the time in prayer and the rest reading the Bible. Remember to ask the Lord to speak to you through His Word.)

_____

_____

_____

_____

_____

_____

_____

No one can get to know God without spending time with Him.

B. **"I have treasured the words of God's mouth more than my daily bread." "Like newborn babies, crave pure spiritual milk so that by it you may grow."** We need devotions every day or we become spiritually malnourished. But we've learned that *our appetite for the Word depends on our obedience to it.* So each time we read the Scriptures, we ask ourselves, "What does it say?," "What does it mean?," and "What can I do about it today?" (Job 23:12b; 1 Peter 2:2)

1. What brings about spiritual growth in your life?

_____

_____

_____

_____

_____

"[God's] Word is a lamp to my feet and light for my path."
Psalm 119:105

2. Why do you think Satan tries to keep you from reading God's Word?

_____

_____

_____

3. How does it benefit you to realize that growth is gradual rather than instant?

_____

_____

_____

_____

156 *Goal Eight: Devotions*

If you have no desire to read the Bible, are you sure you know the Author?

4. What are some things that can hinder your appetite for God's Word?

_____

_____

_____

_____

_____

5. Choose a Bible verse you like, then answer the following questions:

• Verse:

_____

_____

_____

_____

• What does it say?

_____

_____

_____

_____

Save precious time by skipping your devotions.
Signed,
Satan

• What does it mean?

_____

_____

_____

_____

• What can I do about it today?

_____

_____

_____

_____

C. We rely on the Bible to teach us who we are. **"Therefore, if anyone is in Christ, he is a new [person]; the old has gone, the new has come! All this is from God, who [brought us into harmony with] Himself through Christ."** As we renew our minds by reading God's Word, we

Goal Eight: Devotions 157

discover His plan for our lives. **"Be [changed] by the renewing of your mind. Then you will be able to test and [prove] what God's will is— His good, pleasing, and perfect will."** (2 Corinthians 5:17; Romans 12:2)

1. Who are you in Christ? (See pages 95-96; or if you don't know Him, see pages 15-39.)

_____

_____

_____

_____

_____

> It's hard to hear God's "still small voice" with the TV going, the radio blaring and the phone ringing. Try the "off" button and enjoy your quiet time.
> Gwen Shamblin

2. How do you know for sure that you are a new person?

_____

_____

_____

_____

3. What difference does being a new person make in your daily life?

_____

_____

_____

_____

_____

4. How can you renew your mind?

_____

_____

_____

_____

> A wise person is never too busy to spend time with God.

5. For what reasons do you need to renew your mind each day?

_____

_____

_____

_____

_____

D. The Lord Himself lives within us, so we are never alone. Each morning we talk with Him as our dearest friend and seek His wisdom. **"If any of you lacks wisdom, he should ask God, who gives generously to all without finding fault, and it will be given to him."** Following God's guidance prevents frustration and foolish decisions. Throughout our day and at bedtime, we talk things over with the Lord. We share our needs, hurts, and secret desires with Him. **"Delight yourself in the Lord, and He will give you the desires of your heart."** (James 1:5; Psalm 37:4)

1. How does knowing that the Lord lives within you help you make it through the day?

> "The Lord is close to the broken-hearted and saves those who are crushed in spirit."
> Psalm 34:18

2. How can you be sure that it's okay to share your hurts (or whatever you're feeling) with the Lord?

3. What need, hurt, or desire have you recently shared with the Lord?

4. How can you claim God's promise in Psalm 37:4 (above)?

> Give all He asks, and take all He promises.
> S. D. Gordon

Goal Eight: Devotions 159

5. What does it mean to **"Delight yourself in the Lord"**?

_____

_____

_____

_____

_____

Prayer asks and praise takes (obtains the answer).
Don Gossett

E. We remember to pray for others as well as ourselves. Asking the Lord for the needs of others helps release us from bitterness and self-centeredness. When making prayer requests, we yield our will to God. We praise Him that He is in control and will answer in His time, in His way. **"Do not be anxious about anything, but in everything by prayer and petition, with thanksgiving, present your requests to God." "Cast all your [worries] on Him because He cares for you."** (Philippians 4:6; 1 Peter 5:7)

1. What are some benefits of praying for others, especially those whom you resent?

_____

_____

_____

_____

_____

2. Why is it necessary to yield your will when making prayer requests?

_____

_____

_____

_____

_____

"We do not know what we ought to pray for but the Spirit Himself [prays] for us with groans that words cannot express."
Romans 8:26b

3. What if you don't know how to pray? (See page 205.)

_____

_____

_____

_____

_____

160   _Goal Eight: Devotions_

4. God always answers prayer with "yes," "no," or "wait." What might be some reasons for a "wait" answer?

_____

_____

_____

_____

_____

God's promises are notes drawn upon the bank of faith.

5. Why do you think praise and thanksgiving are such a vital part of prayer?

_____

_____

_____

_____

_____

Evaluate Your Progress
(To be discussed with your sponsor-mentor as well as written below.)

Lasting change comes by letting the Lord work through you to accomplish each Goal. How has your life or thinking changed as a result of focusing on Goal Eight?

_____

_____

_____

_____

_____

_____

_____

_____

_____

_____

_____

_____

_____

"Let us throw off everything that hinders and the sin that so easily entangles us, and let us run with perseverance the race marked out for us."
Hebrews 12:1b

Goal Eight: Devotions 161

Notes

> Our days are so booked with frantic activity that we schedule God right out of our days, then wonder why our Christianity is so weak and powerless.

162 *Goal Eight: Devotions*

Goal Nine: Fellowship

Fellowship helps us battle the storms of life.

A. **WE MAINTAIN FELLOWSHIP WITH THE LORD AND THOSE FRIENDS WHO SUPPORT OUR RECOVERY.** We realize that we become like those with whom we spend our time. Therefore, we fellowship with the Lord and the people who love Him. **"Do not set foot on the path of the wicked or walk in the way of evil men. Avoid it, do not travel on it; turn from it, and go your way."** We choose our friends with care because **"he who walks with the wise grows wise, but a companion of fools suffers harm."** (Proverbs 4:14–15; 13:20)

1. What are some reasons to choose your companions carefully?

   _____
   _____
   _____
   _____
   _____

2. In what ways can companions influence your life?

   _____
   _____
   _____
   _____
   _____
   _____
   _____

Show me your friends, and I will show you your future.

3. How can you determine whether a friendship is healthy?

   _____
   _____
   _____
   _____
   _____
   _____

4. Why does letting Christ live through you make you closer to some people and further from others?

   _____
   _____

Goal Nine: Fellowship

_____

_____

_____

NOTE: Question five below should not be discussed in group.

5. Who are your companions, and what influence does each one have in your life? *(Use first names only, and do not share your answer with anyone except a counselor or sponsor whom you trust.)*

> Spiritual growth cannot occur in a vacuum. We must interact with other members of the body.

_____

_____

_____

_____

_____

_____

_____

_____

_____

B. Sin will interrupt our *fellowship* with the Lord, but it cannot change our *relationship.* We're always God's dearly loved children, and it hurts Him when we disobey. *The tragedy of sin isn't that we break rules but that we break hearts.* We grieve our dear Lord and cause heartache for ourselves and others. To fellowship with God and our Christian friends, we cannot allow sin to rule our lives. **"If we walk in the light as [Christ] is in the light, we have fellowship with one another…"** Ceasing to enjoy daily devotions or the company of other Christians usually means that we have allowed sin or misbeliefs to control our lives. (1 John 1:7)

1. Once you have become God's child, how can you be sure He will never disown you or stop loving you?

> "God has said, 'Never will I leave you; never will I forsake you.'"
> Hebrews 13:5b

_____

_____

_____

2. What is so sad about sin?

_____

_____

_____

164   *Goal Nine: Fellowship*

_____

_____

_____

3. What are some misbeliefs that would hinder your desire to fellowship with other Christians?

_____

_____

_____

_____

_____

4. How do your interactions with others reveal your need for spiritual growth?

_____

_____

_____

_____

_____

_____

"Therefore, if you are offering your gift at the altar and there remember that your brother has something against you, leave your gift there in front of the altar. First go and be reconciled to your brother; then come and offer your gift."
Matthew 5:23-24

5. What does the Scripture in the left margin mean to you?

_____

_____

_____

_____

_____

_____

_____

_____

C. To restore fellowship with the Lord and others we've offended, we admit our wrong and turn from it. **"He who covers his sin shall not prosper, but he who confesses and forsakes it shall have mercy." "If we confess our sins, [God] is faithful and will forgive us... and purify us." "Confess to one another therefore your faults—your slips, your false steps, your offenses, your sins; and pray also for one another, that you may be healed and restored."** (Proverbs 28:13 NKJV; 1 John 1:9; James 5:16 Amplified Bible)

Goal Nine: Fellowship 165

1. When you have broken fellowship with the Lord, how and when can it be restored?

_____
_____
_____
_____
_____

"Whoever loves God must also love his brother."
1 John 4:21b

2. How does your relationship with the Lord affect your attitude toward others?

_____
_____
_____
_____
_____

3. When you confess your wrong to the Lord, how can you be sure that He really forgives you?

_____
_____
_____
_____
_____

4. How does admitting your wrongs and turning from them help restore fellowship with others?

Love received and love given is like breathing in and breathing out. It takes both to remain healthy.

_____
_____
_____
_____

NOTE: Number five may be discussed in group but is to be completed on your own.

5. Evaluate your need to make amends on the Action Sheet on the opposite page.

166 *Goal Nine: Fellowship*

Amends Action Sheet*

Just do what you should and leave the results with God. Without excuses or blame, admit what you've done wrong and ask for forgiveness.

Whom I've wronged and how

Look for broken promises, pain you have caused, and people you have hurt by anger, blame, or neglect. You are not responsible for how others may have wronged you, but only for your own behavior.

How I will make amends

Going to the offended person is usually best. Avoid writing a letter unless no other means of contact is possible. If direct contact is impossible, or may cause further harm, make amends indirectly.

One of the best ways to say you're sorry is to change the offending behavior.

*This page may be photocopied for use with the *Overcomer's Handbook*.

Goal Nine: Fellowship 167

The best vitamin for developing friends is B₁.

D. Friendship is a two-way street. To make friends, we practice being one. **"[Lord], I am a friend to all who [respect] You, to all who follow Your [Word]."** The Golden Rule teaches us how to be a real friend: **"Do to others as you would have them do to you."** (Psalm 119:63; Luke 6:31)

> I went out to find a friend
> but could not find one there.
> I went out to be a friend
> and friends were everywhere.
>
> (author unknown)

1. How does being self-centered affect your ability to build friendships?

   _____

   _____

   _____

   _____

   _____

   _____

2. Share a practical example of how the Golden Rule changes how you treat others.

It's easy to make a mountain out of a mole hill. Just add dirt (gossip).

   _____

   _____

   _____

   _____

   _____

   _____

3. What qualities do you look for in a friend?

   _____

   _____

   _____

   _____

   _____

   _____

4. What are you doing to let the Lord make you into the person you've just described?

   _____

   _____

168   *Goal Nine: Fellowship*

_____

_____

_____

_____

5. What are you doing to encourage fellowship between fellow Overcomers? (Why not plan an activity with your group, or send an encouraging note or testimony to Overcomers in Christ.)

_____

_____

_____

_____

_____

_____

> God's children are members of His body. "The eye cannot say to the hand, 'I don't need you!' and the head cannot say to the feet, 'I don't need you!' on the contrary, those parts of the body that seem to be weaker are indispensable."
> 1 Corinthians 12:21-22

E. To worship the Lord and enjoy Christian fellowship, we actively involve ourselves in a Bible-believing church. **"Let us not give up meeting together as some are in the habit of doing, but let us encourage one another…"** Lone-wolf Christianity is foreign to the Bible and puts us in danger of backsliding. Some of our greatest blessings come through fellowship in a local church. **"Accept one another, just as Christ has accepted you, in order to bring praise to God."** (Hebrews 10:25; Romans 15:7)

1. What are some good reasons for involving yourself in a Bible-believing church?

_____

_____

_____

_____

_____

_____

2. If you feel uncomfortable in church, why not just "go it alone"?

_____

_____

_____

_____

_____

_____

Goal Nine: Fellowship 169

3. How can you recognize a good church? (No church names please. Instead, share guidelines by which to measure any church. See "Choosing A Church Family" on pages 206-207.)

_____

_____

_____

_____

_____

_____

_____

_____

_____

_____

> Your church is
> like a bank—
> the more you
> put in, the more
> interest you gain.
> John Baker

4. What are some ways you can participate in your church?

_____

_____

_____

_____

_____

_____

_____

> "Encourage one
> another daily."
> Hebrews 3:13

5. What can you do to encourage others in your church?

_____

_____

_____

_____

_____

_____

_____

_____

Evaluate Your Progress

(To be discussed with your sponsor-mentor as well as written below.)

Lasting change comes by letting the Lord work through you to accomplish each Goal. How has your life or thinking changed as a result of focusing on Goal Nine?

_____

_____

_____

_____

_____

_____

_____

_____

_____

_____

_____

_____

_____

> "Let us throw off everything that hinders and the sin that so easily entangles us, and let us run with perseverance the race marked out for us."
>
> Hebrews 12:1b

Notes

Goal Nine: Fellowship 171

Notes

When you feel
dog tired at
night, could it
be because you
growled all day?
John Baker

GOAL TEN: INVENTORY

God's Word mirrors our true condition.

A. **WE KEEP A PERSONAL INVENTORY AND ALLOW THE LORD TO REMOVE OUR DEFECTS.** "Anyone who listens to the Word but does not [take action] is like a person who looks at his face in a mirror and… goes away and immediately forgets what he looks like." The Word of God is like a mirror that reveals our condition. As we begin to take inventory, we pray: "Search me, O God, and know my heart; test my thoughts. Point out anything You find in me that makes You sad…" (James 1:23–24; Psalm 139:23–24 LB)

1. What are some reasons to take an inventory?

   _____
   _____
   _____
   _____
   _____
   _____
   _____

2. How do you feel about taking a personal inventory?

   _____
   _____
   _____
   _____

You never have to worry about being misunderstood by the Lord. He knows you better than you know yourself.

3. How will you benefit by allowing the Lord to search your heart?

   _____
   _____
   _____
   _____

4. In what ways does the Lord's love make it easier to let Him search your heart?

   _____
   _____

Goal Ten: Inventory 173

_____

_____

_____

_____

5. Why should you allow the Lord to search others' hearts rather than take inventory for them?

_____

_____

_____

_____

_____

_____

Personal inventory gives God the opportunity to point out areas of our lives that need to change.

B. Christ removed our sins when He died on the cross. Therefore, taking inventory isn't for the purpose of condemning ourselves. **"There is now no condemnation for those who are in Christ Jesus."** God's Spirit within assures us that we are no longer condemned. However, He gently reminds us when our attitudes and actions grieve the Lord. A lack of inner peace tells us that our behavior or thoughts need to be changed. (Romans 8:1a)

1. How can you avoid feeling condemned when taking inventory?

_____

_____

_____

_____

_____

"The lamp of the Lord searches the spirit of a man; it searches out his inmost being."
Proverbs 20:27

2. What is the work of the Holy Spirit within you?

_____

_____

_____

_____

_____

3. Why do you sometimes cling to wrong behavior rather than let the Lord change you?

_____

_____

_____

_____

_____

> Any sin that we overlook or excuse gives Satan a foothold in our lives.

4. What personal attitude or behavior disturbs your inner peace?

_____

_____

_____

_____

_____

_____

5. After asking God to change you, what is your responsibility?

_____

_____

_____

_____

_____

C. Knowing that **"the heart is deceitful above all things,"** we're careful not to deceive ourselves. Overlooking or excusing sin leads to more sin and bondage. Therefore, we allow the Scriptures to expose our wrong actions and the false beliefs behind them. **"The Word of God is living and active… it judges the thoughts and attitudes of the heart."** Replacing our misbeliefs with God's truth is the secret to lasting change. (Jeremiah 17:9a; Hebrews 4:12)

1. In what way does the Scripture in the left margin expose any wrong actions and/or misbeliefs you may have?

_____

_____

_____

_____

_____

> "Everyone should be quick to listen, slow to speak, and slow to become angry, for man's anger does not bring about the righteous life that God desires."
> James 1:19b-20

Goal Ten: Inventory 175

2. What excuses have you used to avoid dealing with problems?

_____

_____

_____

_____

_____

_____

What we believe about God and ourselves will determine our behavior.

3. How do misbeliefs lead to wrong actions?

_____

_____

_____

_____

_____

4. How can you overcome your misbeliefs?

_____

_____

_____

_____

_____

5. When inventory reveals many problem areas, what can you do to avoid feeling discouraged?

_____

_____

_____

_____

_____

"And let us not get tired of doing what is right, for after awhile we will reap a harvest of blessing if we don't get discouraged and give up."
Galatians 6:9 TLB

D. In examining our behavior, we remember that performance doesn't determine our value to God. Because He paid so much for us, we are His prize possession. When God disciplines, He does it in love to help us become more like Christ. Though He may not approve of what we do, He

176   *Goal Ten: Inventory*

always loves us. **"I am convinced that neither death nor life, neither angels nor demons, neither the present nor the future, nor any powers, neither height nor depth, nor anything else in all creation will be able to separate us from the love of God that is in Christ Jesus our Lord."** (Romans 8:38–39)

1. How do you know you are God's prize possession?

God loves us just as we are, but too much to let us stay that way.

2. What are the things which *cannot* separate you from God's love?

3. How does God's unchanging love affect the way you look at personal failure or success?

God's purpose for our lives is that we become more like Christ.

4. Why does the Lord discipline?

Goal Ten: Inventory 177

5. How do you respond when your disobedience to God's Word forces Him to discipline you?

_____

_____

_____

_____

_____

_____

To be rightly related to those around you, you must be rightly related to God.

E. We keep an ongoing inventory and talk it over with a loving God. When we discover behavior that is not Christ-like, we promptly admit our wrong. Then, we ask the Lord to change us rather than relying on our own power. God's Word reminds us, **"After beginning with the Spirit [of God], are you now trying to [reach] your goal by human effort?"** Building our new life isn't a "do-it-yourself" project. **"I can do everything *through Him* who gives me strength."** (Galatians 3:3; Philippians 4:13)

IMPORTANT: Do a personal inventory (pages 180-182) before answering the questions below.

1. What areas has the Lord helped you improve?

_____

_____

_____

_____

_____

2. What problems are you turning over to Him?

_____

_____

_____

_____

_____

You can say, "I can't," as long as in the next breath you say, "But God, You can."
Kay Arthur

3. With the Lord's help, what relationship will you work on?

_____

_____

_____

_____

178 *Goal Ten: Inventory*

Christ-likeness comes as we allow Him to control our thoughts and actions.

4. What action will you take to become more Christ-like?

_____

_____

_____

_____

_____

5. What are your thoughts after talking over your inventory with the Lord?

_____

_____

_____

_____

_____

Evaluate Your Progress
(To be discussed with your sponsor-mentor as well as written below.)

Lasting change comes by letting the Lord work through you to accomplish each Goal. How has your life or thinking changed as a result of focusing on Goal Ten?

_____

_____

_____

_____

_____

_____

_____

_____

_____

_____

_____

_____

"Let us throw off everything that hinders and the sin that so easily entangles us, and let us run with perseverance the race marked out for us."
Hebrews 12:1b

Goal Ten: Inventory 179

Personal Inventory (Misbeliefs)

If the enemy can't puff you up with pride, he will try to dampen your spirit by discouragement. It's his best tool.

Check the thoughts below which you believe.

- ☐ There's no hope.
- ☐ Others can be happy, but I can't.
- ☐ I must have the approval of others.
- ☐ I don't have time for devotions.
- ☐ God doesn't answer my prayers.
- ☐ I don't need anyone but myself.
- ☐ Others are to blame for my behavior.
- ☐ I don't have anything worthwhile.
- ☐ I should be able to have what I want.
- ☐ I can't afford to give anything to God.
- ☐ Things must be done my way or not at all.
- ☐ Those who don't live up to my expectations deserve my anger.
- ☐ If I stuff my feelings, they'll go away.
- ☐ I am completely alone—even God has deserted me.
- ☐ Christians shouldn't have problems.
- ☐ I don't need to love those who treat me wrongly.
- ☐ I can't help acting the way I do.
- ☐ I have no choice.
- ☐ My thoughts need to center around myself.
- ☐ When I get angry, I'm not responsible for what I say or do.
- ☐ Nobody cares about me.
- ☐ My behavior and what others think of me determine my value.
- ☐ I can't change.

Above all, we must take responsibility for our thought life.

If you want your life to change for good, this mental garbage must be thrown out. You can find the truth with which to replace this "stinkin' thinkin'" in God's Word.

Personal Inventory (Attitude and Behavior)

Compare the qualities on the left with those on the right. Ask the Lord to reveal the truth to you, then check the box which best describes you today. If you discover many unChrist-like areas, you may need to repeat the Steps to Freedom on pages 45-96.

Christ-likeness comes from the inside out as we let Him control every area of our life.

Christ-like			UnChrist-like
Honesty			Denial
Forgiving			Resentful
Faith			Worry
Humility			Pride
Gentle			Harsh
Appreciate time alone			Dread to be alone
Pure (clean)			Impure (filthy)
Caring about others			Self-centered
Confident			Insecure
Loving			Hateful
Joy-filled			Complaining
Peaceful			Troubled
Kind			Unkind
Patient			Impatient
Self-controlled			Uncontrolled
Responsible			Irresponsible
Doing things on time			Putting things off
Focused on goals			Confused and drifting
Giving			Selfish
Encouraging others			Fault-finding, critical
Calm			Tense
Standing for what is right			Compromising what is right
Caring enough to confront			Enabling unhealthy behavior
Thankful			Ungrateful
Content			Restless
Slow to anger			Quick-tempered
Tolerant of others			Easily offended
Hard working			Lazy

Goal Ten: Inventory

Personal Inventory * *(Goals)*

Neglecting a single Goal will threaten your progress. Check the Goals you are reaching, and put an X by those you need to allow the Lord to work on.

☐ 1. We face the truth knowing that TRUTH forms our lifeline to recovery.

☐ 2. We choose a positive ATTITUDE because attitudes lead to action.

☐ 3. We practice Christ-honoring habits one day at a time to build our HEALTH.

☐ 4. We find freedom to determine our destiny by making wise DECISIONS.

☐ 5. We put our FAITH in Jesus Christ who is the source of inner peace.

☐ 6. We forgive others as we experience and appreciate God's FORGIVENESS

☐ 7. We SURRENDER our will to discover God's plan for our lives.

☐ 8. We make time for daily DEVOTIONS so God can transform our lives.

☐ 9. We maintain FELLOWSHIP with the Lord and those friends who support our recovery.

☐ 10. We keep a personal INVENTORY and allow the Lord to remove our defects.

☐ 11. We transfer our dependency to God to claim the VICTORY that is ours in Christ.

☐ 12. We gratefully OUTREACH by sharing the message of victory in Christ.

If you aim to go nowhere, you're sure to get there.

There are only two reasons why a Christian fails:

1. He does not know who he is in Christ.
2. He forgets it.   T. L. Osborn

*Pages 180-182 may be photocopied for use with the *Overcomer's Handbook*.

Goal Eleven: Victory

"Those who hope in the Lord will soar like eagles."
Isaiah 40:31

A. **We Transfer Our Dependency to God to Claim the Victory that is Ours In Christ.** In the past, we've been dependent on people and things for our self-worth and identity. Now we know that only God can fully meet our needs. **"My God will meet all your needs according to His riches in Christ Jesus."** As we depend on Him, we experience His power and inner peace. If we lean on people instead of the Lord, we not only fail to mature, but we limit ourselves to human resources. Jesus said, **"Without me, you can do nothing."** (Philippians 4:19; John 15:5c NKJV)

1. Whom or what do you most often think and talk about?

   _____
   _____
   _____

2. Whom do you turn to first to meet your needs?

   _____
   _____
   _____

3. Whom are you most concerned about pleasing, and why? (Your honest answers to questions one through three will help you determine whether you're really depending on the Lord.)

   _____
   _____
   _____
   _____
   _____
   _____
   _____

God wants the members of His body to be interdependent not independent or co-dependent.

4. What are the dangers of living to please people rather than the Lord?

   _____
   _____
   _____
   _____
   _____
   _____

Goal Eleven: Victory 183

> "Faith by itself,
> if it is not
> accompanied
> by action,
> is dead."
> James 2:17

5. In what ways does depending on the Lord require you to take action?

_____
_____
_____
_____
_____

B. The path to victory is paved with mistakes. Being accepted by God doesn't hinge on whether we blunder. We learn from our mistakes and turn them over to Him. **"When I am weak, then I am strong [through Christ]."** The Lord doesn't give up on us even though others might. **"I am sure that God who began a good work within you will keep right on helping you grow in His grace until His task within you is finally finished on that day when Jesus Christ returns."** (2 Corinthians 12:10b; Philippians 1:6 TLB)

1. What are some specific things you can do to learn from your mistakes?

_____
_____
_____
_____
_____

2. When you fail, how can you avoid the tendency to doubt God's love?

_____
_____
_____
_____
_____

> Falling down
> doesn't make
> you a failure,
> but staying
> down does.

3. What is one thing you've learned from past mistakes?

_____
_____
_____
_____
_____

184 *Goal Eleven: Victory*

Need strength?
"The JOY OF THE LORD is your strength."
Neh. 8:10

4. What does, **"When I am weak, then I am strong."** mean to you?

_____

_____

_____

_____

_____

_____

_____

_____

5. What daily blessings has the Lord given to prove His love and care for you?

_____

_____

_____

_____

_____

_____

_____

_____

_____

_____

_____

_____

What you think about most reveals who occupies the throne of your heart.

C. Through yielding to Christ living in us, we gain victory over sin and Satan. Satan can't get our souls, but he tries to ruin our lives by putting wrong thoughts in our minds. Jesus used the Scriptures as a weapon against Satan's lies, and so do we. **"The Word of God is living and active, sharper than any double-edged sword…" "[Yield] yourselves then to God. Resist the devil* and he will flee from you." "The One who is in you is greater than the one who is in the world."** (Hebrews 4:12; James 4:7; 1 John 4:4b)

*If you've been involved in the occult or suspect demonic oppression, you may need an experienced encourager to help you go through the Steps to Freedom on pages 45-96.

Goal Eleven: Victory 185

1. What are some practical results from realizing Christ actually lives within you?

_____

_____

_____

_____

_____

_____

2. Why is it so important for you to take responsibility for your thought life?

_____

_____

_____

_____

_____

_____

> "We take captive every thought to make it obedient to Christ."
> 2 Corinthians 10:5b

3. What are some of the lies Satan uses to try to defeat you?

_____

_____

_____

_____

_____

4. What are some practical ways to resist Satan?

_____

_____

_____

_____

_____

_____

> Don't think more about your problems than about the Scripture promise you are standing on.
> Gordon Bippas

NOTE: Number five may be discussed in group but is to be completed on your own.

5. Write a verse of God's truth which applies to one of your problem areas in the space below AND on a small card. Then write Satan's lie

186 *Goal Eleven: Victory*

If you correct yourself, God won't need to.

about the problem. Put the card where you can read it (aloud if possible) whenever the lie comes into your mind. This simple plan will help you apply the Scriptures to your misbeliefs so you can overcome them. For example, if anger is your problem, your card might say—

God's truth: **"In your anger do not sin. Do not let the sun go down while you are still angry, and do not give the devil a foothold."** (Ephesians 4:26–27)

Satan's lie: "I can't help the way I act when I get mad."

God's truth:

_____

_____

_____

_____

Satan's lie:

_____

_____

_____

_____

"Rebellion is like the sin of [witchcraft] and arrogance like the evil of [idol worship]."
1 Samuel 15:23

D. There are no rebels in the ranks of the victorious. To experience victory, we cooperate with the Lord by obeying His Word. Obedience is our response to His overwhelming love. **"If you love me, you will obey what I command."** Obedience to Christ means letting Him control every part of our bodies, including our minds and our mouths. **"Live by the Spirit and you will not [give in to] the desires of the sinful nature." "We died to sin; how can we live in it any longer?"** Formerly, we were controlled by our compulsive behavior. What a relief to be controlled by God's Spirit! (John 14:15; Galatians 5:16; Romans 6:2b)

1. What practical difference does it make when you realize that you are dead to sin?

_____

_____

_____

Goal Eleven: Victory 187

> If the *problem* becomes the focus, it will never go away. If the *solution* becomes the focus, the problem will fade away.
> Marie Schilling

2. What attitudes and actions would indicate that you're not letting Christ live through you? Be specific.

_____

_____

_____

_____

_____

3. What practical changes will result from allowing Christ to have full control of your body?

_____

_____

_____

_____

_____

4. What specific action do you need to take today to obey the Lord?

_____

_____

_____

_____

_____

5. If you do not take the action you just described, what will be the result?

_____

_____

_____

_____

_____

> Is your God a spare tire or a steering wheel?

E. Either constant busyness or frequent idleness sets us up for a fall. Therefore, we use our time wisely. Victory comes one day at a time as we claim God's promises and obey His Word. We plan and set goals, but we do not take on tomorrow's problems or face the future with fear. **"Do not worry about tomorrow, for tomorrow will worry about itself. Each day has enough [problems] of its own." "And we know that all things work together for good to those who love God..."** (Matthew 6:34; Romans 8:28 NKJV)

> "If you think you are standing firm, be careful that you don't fall."
> 1 Corinthians 10:12

1. What's the danger of thinking that you cannot fall into life controlling habits?

_____

_____

_____

_____

_____

2. In what ways can failing to use your time wisely lead to trouble?

_____

_____

_____

_____

_____

_____

3. What are some advantages of using a written "to do" list to plan your time?

_____

_____

_____

_____

_____

4. How can setting personal goals help you?

_____

_____

_____

_____

_____

_____

> Set your goals in your "prayer closet."

Goal Eleven: Victory 189

Going through life without any goals is like riding a merry-go-round. The only direction you can go is in circles.

5. What personal goals do you feel the Lord is prompting you to accomplish within the next twelve months? (Write out no more than three to five goals in the space below. Later copy them into your planner or somewhere that you'll see them often. Keeping your goals visible will remind you to do something toward them every day.)

_____

_____

_____

_____

_____

_____

_____

_____

_____

Evaluate Your Progress
(To be discussed with your sponsor-mentor as well as written below.)

Lasting change comes by letting the Lord work through you to accomplish each Goal. How has your life or thinking changed as a result of focusing on Goal Eleven?

_____

_____

_____

_____

_____

_____

_____

_____

_____

_____

_____

_____

"Let us throw off everything that hinders and the sin that so easily entangles us, and let us run with perseverance the race marked out for us."
Hebrews 12:1b

190   *Goal Eleven: Victory*

GOAL TWELVE: OUTREACH

A. **WE GRATEFULLY OUTREACH BY SHARING THE MESSAGE OF VICTORY IN CHRIST.** We show our gratitude by sharing what has been given to us. When we help others, we help ourselves because *we only keep what we give away.* Jesus said, **"Whoever wants to save his life will lose it, but whoever [gives] his life for me and [shares the good news] will save it." "It is more blessed to give than to receive."** (Mark 8:35, Acts 20:35)

1. For what reasons can you be especially helpful to people who struggle with problems similar to those you've overcome?

   _____
   _____
   _____
   _____
   _____
   _____

By reaching out to others, we help ourselves.

2. What do the Bible verses in section A (bold type) mean to you?

   _____
   _____
   _____
   _____
   _____
   _____
   _____

3. Why is giving absolutely essential to your personal growth?

   _____
   _____
   _____
   _____
   _____

He is no fool who gives what he cannot keep to gain what he cannot lose.
— Jim Elliott

4. In what ways is it more blessed to give than to receive?

   _____
   _____
   _____
   _____

_____
_____

"Carry each
other's burdens
and in this way,
you will fulfill the
law of Christ."
Galatians 6:2

5. What are some specific ways you can use your time and money to help others?

_____
_____
_____
_____
_____

B. **"Each of you should look not only to your own interests, but also to the interests of others."** Reaching out to hurting people plays a vital role in our lives. We're open about our struggles so others realize that we understand their pain. When people want recovery, we share how to become Overcomers in Christ. We also willingly sponsor and disciple others. Sponsorship does as much for us as it does for them. (Philippians 2:4)

1. What are the benefits of being open about your struggles?

_____
_____
_____
_____

Be kind.
Remember that
everyone you
meet is fighting
a hard battle.
Harry Thompson

2. How does meeting the needs of others help you follow the example Jesus set?

_____
_____
_____
_____

3. What can you do to encourage someone who is hurting?

_____
_____
_____
_____

4. How can you determine whom to help and how much?

It is in the storm
that God equips
us for service.

5. How can you help people feel at home in your group? (If you don't have a support group, why not ask your church or sponsor-mentor about getting one started.)

"Dear friends, do not be surprised at the painful trial you are suffering as though something strange were happening to you. But rejoice that you participate in the sufferings of Christ."
1 Peter 4:12-13

C. By letting Christ live through us, we not only "talk the talk," we "walk the walk." Our changed lives either draw people to Him or cause them to turn away. We allow God's love to flow through us and avoid a self-righteous attitude. Christ-like love often wins people when nothing else works. **"Love is patient, love is kind. It does not envy, it does not boast, it is not proud. It is not rude, it is not self-seeking, it is not easily angered, it keeps no record of wrongs. Love does not delight in evil but rejoices with the truth, always hopes, [never gives up]. Love never fails."** (1 Corinthians 13:4–8a)

1. What will result when you allow Christ to live through you?

Goal Twelve: Outreach 193

When people reject Christ, we shouldn't take it personally.

2. What can you do when someone you're trying to reach wants nothing to do with Christ?

_____

_____

_____

_____

_____

3. How can you avoid coming across as self-righteous or "preachy"?

_____

_____

_____

_____

_____

4. Read the Bible verses in paragraph C again. In what specific ways does your behavior need to change in order to show Christ-like love?

_____

_____

_____

_____

_____

If you always do what you always do, you'll always get what you always get.

5. How do you feel about giving Christ-like love to someone you don't think deserves it?

_____

_____

_____

_____

_____

D. When doing outreach, we often take along another Overcomer. **"Two are better than one, because they have [better results from] their work; if one falls down, his friend can help him up."** We know that people often deny their need for recovery. Therefore, we allow the consequences of their own actions to wake them up. When appropriate, we lovingly confront others to help them face reality. We also set boundaries so that we don't participate in their unhealthy behavior. (Ecclesiastes 4:9–10)

> "Speaking the truth in love, we will in all things grow up into Him who is the Head, that is, Christ."
> Ephesians 4:15

1. Why is it usually wise to take along another Overcomer when doing outreach?

_____

_____

_____

_____

_____

2. How does it hurt others when you allow them to take unfair advantage of you?

_____

_____

_____

_____

3. What are the benefits of letting a person feel the consequences of his or her unhealthy behavior?

_____

_____

_____

_____

_____

_____

4. In your own words, what is an intervention? (See definition on page 203.)

_____

_____

_____

_____

_____

_____

_____

_____

> "Gently teach those who oppose the truth. Perhaps... they will come to their senses and escape from the devil's trap."
> 2 Timothy 2:25-26 TNLB

Goal Twelve: Outreach 195

5. What are the dangers of becoming overly concerned about someone else's recovery rather than working on your own issues?

_____

_____

_____

_____

_____

> Jesus said:
> "If the world hates you, keep in mind that it hated me first. If you belonged to the world, it would love you as its own... but I have chosen you out of the world."
> John 15:18-19b

E. Our *Overcomer's Handbook* helps us apply God's Word to our daily walk. By bringing the Lord into every interest and activity, we experience life to the full. Even though the world may hate us, we cannot risk shutting the Lord out of any area of our lives. Satan, the world, and our own flesh will to try to enslave us. But we overcome by claiming the victory Christ already won at the cross. **"We are more than conquerors through Him who loved us."** (Romans 8:37b)

1. What are the three enemies that will try to enslave you and how?

_____

_____

_____

_____

_____

_____

2. How can you bring the Lord into every interest and activity?

_____

_____

_____

_____

_____

_____

_____

_____

_____

_____

> God does not ask about our ability but about our availability.

196 *Goal Twelve: Outreach*

3. What's wrong with keeping the "God part" of your life separate from the rest of it?

Continue working on the Goals, making them a lifelong habit. Remember, what you practice, you become.

4. In what ways has your life changed as a result of your relationship with Jesus Christ?

"If I have a faith that can move mountains, but have not love, I am nothing."
1 Corinthians 13:2

5. In what practical ways can you let Christ's love shine through you to reach others for Him?

Goal Twelve continues on the following page.

Goal Twelve: Outreach 197

Evaluate Your Progress
(To be discussed with your sponsor-mentor as well as written below.)

Lasting change comes by letting the Lord work through you to accomplish each Goal. How has your your life or thinking changed as a result of focusing on Goal Twelve?

_____

_____

_____

_____

_____

_____

_____

_____

_____

_____

_____

_____

_____

"Let us throw off everything that hinders and the sin that so easily entangles us, and let us run with perseverance the race marked out for us."
Hebrews 12:1b

Notes

198 *Goal Twelve: Outreach*

THE OVERCOMER'S COVENANT IN CHRIST

Jesus Christ received is recovery begun. Jesus Christ cherished is recovery advancing. But Jesus Christ controlling every area of life is recovery realized.

1. I place all my trust and confidence in the Lord, and I put no confidence in the flesh. I declare myself to be dependent upon God.

2. I consciously and deliberately choose to submit to God and resist the devil by denying myself, picking up my cross daily and following Jesus.

3. I choose to humble myself before the mighty hand of God in order that He may exalt me at the proper time.

4. I declare the truth that I have died with Christ and was raised with Him. Therefore, I am dead to sin, freed from it, and alive to God.

5. I gladly embrace the truth that I am now a child of God who is unconditionally loved and accepted.

6. I declare that sin shall no longer be master over me because I am not under the law but under grace. There is no more guilt or condemnation because I am spiritually alive in Christ Jesus.

7. I renounce every unrighteous use of my body, and I commit myself to no longer be conformed to this world. Rather, I will be transformed by the renewing of my mind through the Word of God. I choose to believe the truth and walk in it, regardless of my feelings or circumstances.

8. I commit myself to take every thought captive to the obedience of Christ, and choose to think upon that which is true, honorable, right, pure and lovely.

9. I commit myself to God's great goal for my life to conform me to His image.

10. I choose to adopt the attitude of Christ which has nothing to do with selfishness or empty conceit. With humility of mind, I regard others as more important than myself. I do not merely look out for my own interests, but also the interests of others.

Neil T. Anderson and Mike Quarles
adapted

The Overcomer's Covenant In Christ

Notes

Service is
nothing but
love in work
clothes.
John Baker

Section Six

MARATHON ESSENTIALS:
Important Helps

Those who hope in the Lord

will soar like eagles. Isaiah 40:31

- Meanings That Matter
- Understanding The Bible
- Power Through Prayer
- Choosing A Church Family
- Seeking Additional Help
- Avoiding Relapse
- Recommended Resources

MEANINGS THAT MATTER

*Say What?
If you said what
I think you said,
you must not
mean what I
think you mean
—if you know
what I mean.*

Addiction is the habitual use of any substance or activity that interrupts the function of life as God intends it. The purpose may be to gain pleasure or avoid pain, but the result is progressive loss of control. Addiction is self-worship because we make an idol out of our desires instead of centering our lives around Christ.

Born again means to enter God's family by a spiritual birth. Whenever there is a birth, there is life. We are born again when we come to God as a sinner and accept His free gift of eternal life. By faith, we become God's child and take on a whole new identity. Being born again begins a permanent relationship with Jesus Christ as our Savior and Lord. (See Section Two, "The Starting Line," for more information.)

Codependency means addiction to others—that is, dependency on their approval for our sense of well-being and identity. It involves controlling or rescuing others in an attempt to fix their problems without appropriate effort on their part to assume responsibility. Codependency also includes allowing others to control our emotions and actions. The codependent person lacks personal boundaries and makes it easy for others to continue unhealthy behavior.

Cross-talk is conversation during a meeting directed to an individual rather than the entire group. Cross-talk is to be avoided because it often becomes advice giving and fixing.

Cross-addiction means the body's ability to substitute one chemical or compulsive behavior for another to achieve the desired fix. For example, abstaining alcoholics often become sugar addicts. In fact, they were likely addicted to sugar and caffeine before they turned to alcohol. Because of cross-addiction, addicts (or former addicts) who use mood-altering chemicals risk relapse. (People with a chemical imbalance should seek professional help.)

*Our understand-
ing of recovery
terms will depend
on whether we
have a Christ-
centered or
self-centered
worldview.*

Denial is a false system of beliefs not based on reality. It is like having an elephant sitting in our living room that we refuse to acknowledge or talk about. Denial prevents recovery and isolates us from God and the people around us.

Detaching with love involves letting a person feel the consequences of his or her unhealthy behavior. It means firmness without anger or pleading. By detaching with love, we can work on our own issues regardless of what the other person does.

Dysfunctional means damaged and unhealthy. The dysfunctional person fails to handle daily life and relationships as God intends. From His perspective, if we fail to love God with all our heart and our neighbor as ourselves, we are dysfunctional. The degree to which the fruit of the Spirit is evident in our lives also indicates whether we are healthy or dysfunctional.

Healthy self-esteem means seeing ourselves as God sees us—no more, no less. It involves accepting the way God made us while, at the same time, letting Him change us into what He intends us to be. Self-esteem includes both self-worth and self-respect. Self-worth must be based on our acceptance in Christ rather than on performance or the opinion of others. Self respect, however, comes only by doing what we know God would have us to do. We cannot deliberately ignore God's Word and expect to feel good about ourselves.

Interdependence means sharing one another's burdens without depending on each other for identity and self-esteem. Unlike codependency, interdependence involves respect for one another's personal boundaries and responsibilities.

> The world's definition of peace is lack of conflict. God's definition of peace is peace in the conflict.

Intervention is lovingly confronting someone who's out of touch with reality about his or her compulsive behavior. Appropriate consequences for refusing to get help are clearly explained and carried out if necessary. Intervention should not be attempted without an experienced counselor. (See Matthew 18:15–17 for a biblical intervention.)

Recovery means becoming healthy by finding our identity, acceptance, and purpose in the Lord Jesus Christ. Christ-centered recovery is not so much *from* something as *to* Someone. (1 Thess. 1:9) Therefore, we can refer to recovery as spiritual growth. See page 9 for a more complete explanation.

Sin is any attempt to meet our basic needs apart from Christ. Sin has been called man's "Declaration of Independence" from God. We are all born sinners and must be born again to establish a relationship with God and fulfill our destiny. (See definition of "born again" on facing page.)

Sobriety means sane thinking with neither compulsive behavior nor chemicals warping our view of reality. In this broad sense, sobriety relates to all forms of addiction and dysfunction.

Sponsor-mentor refers to someone with *at least two years* in recovery who provides ongoing support and guidance to another person of the same sex. A sponsor must be able to relate to the problems of the person being sponsored. A sponsor can only lead others where he or she has already been. Therefore, a sponsor's walk must match his or her talk. Also, he or she must be willing to lovingly confront when the need arises.

Stress management means learning to handle life's pressures through prayer, reading and obeying God's Word, talking to a friend or counselor, relaxation, and good health habits. A lack of inner peace indicates a need for stress management.

Success is accepting and fulfilling the unique purpose for which God created us. As we use our gifts to serve others, we become fulfilled. We discover our gifts as we walk in the Spirit and interact with other members of the body of Christ.

Meanings That Matter 203

Understanding The Bible

> Reading the Scriptures without putting them into practice is like eating food without digesting it.

1. Seek a relationship with Jesus Christ as your Lord and Savior because *the key to understanding the Bible is knowing the Author.*

2. Continue to read for truth about the Lord Jesus Christ and ways to get to know Him better. He is the central theme of the Bible.

3. Interpret Scriptures in context, and don't use unclear verses to overrule clear ones.

4. Remember that Scripture agrees with Scripture. If it seems to contradict, you are misunderstanding or misapplying it.

5. Take the Bible at face value. While the Scriptures contain some symbols and types, the Bible says what it means and means what it says. So if the first sense makes common sense, seek no other sense.

6. Determine to whom a passage is written to correctly interpret it: believers, unbelievers, or the nation of Israel.

7. Check the meaning of a word in the language in which it was first written by using a Bible concordance. A concordance will also help you locate a particular verse in the Scriptures.

8. Don't expect to understand the whole Bible all at once. Learn a little each day so that you become familiar with Bible terms and teaching. But keep in mind that some of the deeper truths of the Bible won't be fully understood until eternity.

> It's not the Scriptures I don't understand that bother me— it's the ones that I do.
> Mark Twain

9. If you need further help to understand the Bible, ask a born-again* believer who is active in a Bible-believing church. (See pages 206-207 for how to recognize a Bible-believing church.)
   *See the definition of "born again" on page 202.

10. Choose a reliable version of the Bible written in today's English, such as NIV. If possible, use a Bible with study notes to help you apply the Scriptures to daily life. Many people find the Life Application Bible particularly helpful (Zondervan or Tyndale Publishers).

POWER THROUGH PRAYER

Prayer is a process of discovering God's will then asking Him to bring it about. While you can do more than pray, there's nothing more you can do until you have prayed. Here's how to get results:

Nothing is beyond the power of prayer except that which is outside of the will of God.

1. Pray *biblically.* Ask in the name and for the glory of the Lord Jesus Christ. Yield your will to Him.

2. Pray *naturally.* Talking to God doesn't require fancy words or memorized prayers.

3. Pray *respectfully.* God isn't the "guy next door." He's your heavenly Father and your Lord.

4. Pray *purely.* Confess any sin in your life and turn from it. Clinging to sin will prevent God from answering your prayer.

5. Pray *earnestly.* Put your heart into your prayers. Fasting from food or other things may help you focus and avoid distraction.

6. Pray *boldly.* "The devil trembles when he sees the weakest person on their knees."

7. Pray *specifically.* How else will you know when your prayers are answered?

8. Pray *confidently.* "Pray and doubt and do without—pray and believe and receive."

Praise is not optional for the Christian.
Don Gossett

9. Pray *constantly.* Keep on asking until you receive an answer. In addition to regular times of prayer, take advantage of free moments (such as when you are waiting in line).

10. Pray *thankfully.* Remember to continually thank and praise God. That's how you claim His answers to your prayers.

IMPORTANT: Keep in mind that prayer requests from others may be confidential and should not be passed on without their permission.

CHOOSING A CHURCH FAMILY

Choose your church family with care. Look for a church which teaches the basic Bible truths in the O.I.C. Statement of Faith below:

1. The Scriptures are the inspired Word of God and contain no error. They are the authority for our faith, worship, and behavior.
(2 Timothy 3:16–17; 2 Peter 1:20–21; Psalm 119:105)

2. There is one God in three equal persons: God the Father, God the Son, and God the Holy Spirit.
(2 Corinthians 13:14; Matthew 28:19; 2 Corinthians 1:21–22)

3. Jesus Christ is the eternal Son of God, miraculously born of the virgin Mary. He came into the world to save sinners and destroy the works of Satan.
(John 1:1; Matthew 1:18–23; 1 John 3:5 & 8; Col. 1:13-14)

4. God is our Creator; we are His creation. We are made in His image, but we are not our own god. A biblical understanding of God, and who we are in relationship to Him, is foundational to all other life issues.
(Genesis 1:27; Acts 12:21–23; 2 Cor. 5:15)

5. All mankind has sinned. Jesus Christ is the only person who has lived an absolutely sinless life. We can find forgiveness and new life only by becoming God's child through a spiritual rebirth. (See the definition of "born again" on page 174.)
(Romans 3:23; John 3:3; 1 Peter 1:23; John 1:12-13)

6. On the cross, Jesus took the punishment for our sins and satisfied the demands of a holy God. God showed that He accepted this finished work by raising Christ from the dead.
(Isaiah 53:5–6; 1 Peter 2:24; Romans 4:25)

7. By trusting Christ as our sin-bearer, we can be sure of heaven. Through faith, we receive eternal life and acceptance with God as a gift rather than something to be earned.
(Ephesians 2:8–9; Titus 3:5; Acts 16:31)

8. There is one church, the body of Christ, with Him as the head. All who trust Christ as their Savior have the Holy Spirit in their heart and are part of His church.
(1 Corinthians 12:12–13; Ephesians 1:22–23; 4:4–6)

> Jesus said, "My mother and brothers are those who hear God's Word and put it into practice."
> Luke 8:21

> Fellowship with brothers and sisters in Christ gives us a fore-taste of Heaven.

9. All power belongs to Jesus Christ, and Satan has been defeated by Him. However, Satan tries to keep people in bondage so that they will remain ineffective for Christ. Freedom comes by rejecting Satan's lies and walking in the light of God's truth.
(Romans 8:37-38; Ephesians 6:12; James 4:7; John 8:32)

10. Our relationship with God and the people around us indicates our true spiritual condition. To the extent that we fall short of loving the Lord with all our heart, soul, strength and mind, and loving our neighbor as ourselves, we need recovery.
(Matthew 22:37-39; 1 Corinthians 13:1-8; 1 John 4:20-21)

11. Christ will soon come again to catch up all living believers to heaven. Later, Christ will return to establish His earthly kingdom.
(1 Corinthians 15:51–54; 1 Thessalonians 4:13–18; 2 Peter 3:3–9)

12. God will raise from the dead those who accepted Christ during their lifetime and take them to heaven. People who rejected Christ will be raised from the dead to be judged and eternally punished.
(1 Thessalonians 4:13–18; Revelation 20:11–15; John 3:18)

Also, choose a church which:

a. Teaches that a Christ-like walk develops over time rather than occurring instantly.

b. Provides prayer support to help you overcome problems.

c. Preaches loving obedience to God's Word rather than man-made rules.

d. Shows unconditional love, regardless of your income, educational level, or social standing.

e. Encourages people to be real and admit their problems rather than hide them.

f. Provides, or will refer you to, Christ-centered recovery resources.

> Without a church family, this world would be a cold place.

> Real friends are those who, when you've made a fool of yourself, don't feel that you've done a permanent job.

Choosing A Church Family 207

SEEKING ADDITIONAL HELP

Many people have become healthy by following the Christ-centered recovery plan outlined in this Handbook. But if you find yourself unable to progress, you may wish to consider treatment and/or counseling.

CAUTION for those with special needs:
Detoxification from alcohol or drugs requires medical supervision. Also, seek immediate help if you are dangerous to yourself or others.

Choosing a Godly Counselor

> "Blessed is the man who walks not in the counsel of the ungodly."
> Psalm 1:1 NKJV

1. Pray for the Lord's guidance to make the right choice.

2. Ask your church or other ministry whom they recommend. Also ask Christians who are recovered where they found help. (Support groups cannot endorse, so ask members outside of group time.)

3. Choose someone experienced in dealing with your particular problem. (If you can't find anyone who specializes in your area of need, you may find help by reading appropriate books from our "Recommended Resources" on pages 210-212.)

4. Ask the counselor if (s)he uses the Bible in counseling. Look for someone whose counseling agrees with Scripture because mainline psychology will lead you astray.

5. Check the counselor's reputation and credentials.

6. Ask about cost. Some counselors accept a freewill offering, and others charge according to your ability to pay.

Final note: Don't stay indefinitely with a counselor who doesn't seem to help. However, don't look for someone who will go along with your current way of life. Expect to make changes in order to recover.

Locating a Treatment Facility

> Overcomers in Christ—When an unknown god is not enough!

(If someone close to you needs treatment but refuses it, contact a treatment center about an intervention. Do not attempt an intervention without guidance.)

While O.I.C. does not endorse, we can refer you to Christ-centered treatment. If you go to a treatment center that does not hold a biblical point of view, don't attempt to change them. Instead, take what you can use and leave the rest.

208 *Seeking Additional Help*

AVOIDING RELAPSE

Twelve Ways To "Blow It"

Relapse means returning to unhealthy behavior after a period of victory. It includes carelessness about your relationship with the Lord and the people close to you. Another name for relapse is backsliding. You can backslide regardless of how long you have been in recovery. Here's how:

1. Let fear or other negative emotions control you instead of claiming the victory that is yours in Christ.

2. Refuse to take responsibility for your thought life and allow your thoughts to drift wherever they will.

3. Isolate yourself from people who care about your recovery, especially your support group.

4. Don't interact with a sponsor-mentor who might ask questions you'd rather not answer.

5. Stuff your feelings rather than deal with them.

6. Criticize others and blame them for your problems.

7. Carry a "chip on your shoulder" and, when you get mad, stay mad.

8. Focus on "me, myself, and I" instead of living to benefit others.

9. Become overconfident and ignore God's Word and the Overcomer's Goals.

10. Let your guard down whenever you're in a particularly good or bad mood.

11. Overlook or excuse personal sin—nobody's perfect.

12. Indulge in your sin of choice now and then just to prove you can handle it.

> Recovery is like walking up a down escalator. When you stop moving forward, you automatically move backwards.

> He who flees temptation should not leave a forwarding address.

Avoiding Relapse 209

RECOMMENDED RESOURCES

Depending on your particular need, you will find some of the following books helpful. Most can be ordered through Christian bookstores.

You can also benefit from the resources by Dr. Charles Stanley. Contact: In Touch Ministries; P.O. Box 7900; Atlanta, GA 30357; 1-800-323-3747.

Let no book keep you from the best book (the Bible).

An Affair of the Mind (excellent for overcoming porn addiction)
Laurie Hall
Focus on the Family

Angry Men and the Women Who Love Them
(For overcoming abuse and understanding arrested development)
Paul Hegstrom
Beacon Hill Press

Antonomy of a Food Addiction: The Brain Chemisty of Overeating
(Secular, reader discretion advised)
Anne Katherine, M.A.
Gurze Books

Battered Into Submission: Wife Abuse in the Christian Home
James Alsdurf & Phyllis Alsdurf
InterVarsity Press

Bold Love (Practical guidance for overcoming ongoing abuse)
Dan Allender and Tremper Longman III
NavPress

Bondage Breaker: Overcoming Negative Thoughts, Habitual Sins
Neil T. Anderson (The <u>youth</u> version is coauthored by Dave Park)
Harvest House

Boundaries: When to Say Yes, When to Say No to Take Control of Your Life
Cloud and Townsend
Zondervan

Measure all human ideas by God's Word or you will be led astray.

Boundaries for Kids: (How to set boundaries for your children)
Cloud and Townsend
Zondervan

Caffeine Blues: Wake Up To The Hidden Dangers of America's #1Drug
(Secular, reader discretion advised)
Stephen Cherniske, M.S.
Warner Books

Christ-Centered Marriage
Anderson and Mylander
Regal Books

Drugs and Drinking: What Every Teen and Parent Should Know
Jay Strack
Thomas Nelson Publishers

False Intimacy: Understanding the Struggle of Sexual Addiction
Dr. Harry Schaumburg
NavPress

Freedom from Addiction Workbook
Neil T. Anderson with Mike & Julia Quarles
Gospel Light

God is for the Alcoholic
Jerry Dunn & Bernard Palmer
Moody Press

Guide To God: A User-Friendly Approach
(For those who don't yet know the Lord)
Bruce Bickel and Stan Jantz
Harvest House

Healthy Habits: 20 Simple Ways to Improve Your Health
David and Anne Frahm
NavPress

Helping Others Find Freedom In Christ
Neil T. Anderson
Regal Books

Hinds Feet On High Places
(Children's book, but excellent for adult children)
Hannah Hurnard
Destiny Image

How Can I Be Sure I'm a Christian: What the Bible says about assurance
Donald S. Whitney
NavPress

How to Lead Small Groups
Neal McBride
NavPress

If Christ Were Your Counselor
Dr. Chris Thurman
Thomas Nelson Publishers

Lick the Sugar Habit: Sugar addiction upsets your body chemistry
(Secular, reader discretion advised)
Nancy Appleton, Ph.D.
Avery Publishing

Let Us Pray
Watchman Nee
Christian Fellowship Publishers

> "My people are destroyed from lack of knowledge."
> Hosea 4:6

> The road to knowledge begins with the turn of a page.

Recommended Resources 211

Making Ends Meet: Budgeting Made Easy
Larry Burkett with Brenda Armstrong
Christian Financial Concepts

Monster Within (The) (overcoming eating disorders)
Cynthia Rowland
Baker Book House

Overcoming Depression
Neil T. Anderson & Hal Baumchem
Regal Books

Potatoes Not Prozac (how food affects brain chemicals)
(Secular, reader discretion advised)
Kathleen DesMaisons; PH.D., Addictive Nutrition
Simon & Schuster

Seduction Of Our Children
Neil T. Anderson & Steve Russo
Harvest House

Search for Significance (with workbook)
Robert S. McGee
Rapha
Distributed by Word Publishing

Satanic Revival (The)
Mark Bubeck
Here's Life Publishers

Trusting God Even When Life Hurts
Jerry Bridges
NavPress

Victory Over The Darkness: Realizing the Power of Your Identity In Christ
Stomping Out The Darkness (Youth version of above book)
Neil T. Anderson (Youth version co-authored by Dave Park)
Regal Books

What The Bible Says About Healthy Living
Rex Russell, M.D.
Regal Books

Way of Escape, A (sexual addiction recovery)
Neil T. Anderson
Harvest House

You Are Special
(Children's book, but excellent for adult children)
Max Lucado
Crossway Books

Your Money, Frustration or Freedom
Howard Dayton, Jr.
Tyndale House

Knowing without doing is like plowing without sowing.

It takes wisdom to put knowledge into practice.

212 *Recommended Resources*

Section Seven

FELLOW RUNNERS
Testimonies

Those who hope in the Lord will soar like eagles. Isaiah 40:31

- We're Family
- The Overcomers Story
- Member Interviews

We're Family

No matter what I've done or been,
I'm okay.
'Cause I let Jesus take my sins,
so I'm okay.

Since you let Jesus set you free,
you're okay.
God loves you the same as me,
so you're okay.

Since He accepts you, I do too—
we're both okay.
That makes us family, me and you.
Okay?

Because we belong to Christ, we are family to one another.

THE OVERCOMERS (O.I.C.) STORY

When Russ came back into our lives, his slouched shuffle and downcast eyes made him the picture of rejection. But we never guessed that hiding beneath his droopy, oversized coat was a hopeless drug addict, alcoholic, and Satan worshipper.

It was January, 1982. My husband Bill and I were devoted to the Lord and had raised a close, happy family. God was about to give us a painful lesson on addiction we'd never forget!

Russ had been my mother's foster child ten years earlier. I remember him as a loving child who tirelessly helped care for my ailing father.

Two years later, when he thought that his home situation had improved, Russ returned to his parents. But his hopes were soon crushed as again he found himself a victim of addiction's cruelty. His alcoholic father beat him with a bicycle chain and yelled at him to get out.

Although barely 13, Russ found himself homeless. Finding nowhere else to turn, he joined a carnival. There he got deeply into drugs and alcohol to hide his pain. After years of bouncing in and out of trouble and jails, Russ came to us at age 22, suicidal and violent.

When God wants to do something good, He starts with a difficulty. When he wants to do something spectacular, He starts with an impossibility.

Words can't describe the next four years. Looking back brings renewed pain for Russ and ourselves. Because Bill and I knew so little about addiction, Russ soon gained control of our relationship. Our love for him, coupled with a lack of experience, made us easy to manipulate. Unknowingly, we enabled him to continue using. However, the Lord protected, and I believed that He would bring something good out of our nightmare.

Russ became both dependent on us and dangerous. I seemed to be his primary target. Once he threw a knife at me and another time, a large rock. Other instances too painful to describe convinced me that Satan was trying to destroy me.

In time, Bill and I learned about "tough love." It was our only tool to make Russ face his problems. With our encouragement, he tried church, treatment centers, support groups, counselors, and mental hospitals.

But the downward spiral continued. Nothing gave him or us more than temporary relief.

Finally, God spoke loudly to Russ through a nearly fatal motorcycle accident. One month later, in the middle of the night, he trusted Christ as his Savior. But to our dismay, addiction still had a stranglehold on him. He had to be taught how to find victory in Christ one step at a time.

The Overcomers Story

Russ' overwhelming needs required a simple but comprehensive plan dealing with the whole person (spiritual, physical, mental, emotional, and social). I searched desperately for an effective recovery program. Careful research convinced me that the best from many sources needed to be combined into one dynamic, Christ-centered plan.

But who was I to attempt such an awesome task? Yet, how else could people falling through the cracks of traditional treatment find help?

With much prayer and Bill's support, I began to write. My goal was to write a biblically-sound recovery program marked by simplicity and completeness. Jesus Christ, rather than one's self or others, would provide the strength and foundation for recovery.

I began testing the program on Russ over the phone to avoid his radical mood changes. His input kept the needs and viewpoint of the addicted foremost. I rewrote and retested again and again. What a challenge to teach him how to walk in the light of his new identity in Christ!

A "god as we understand him" is never quite big enough!

Gradually, Russ began to recover. As his addiction lost its hold, we all began to live a more normal life. Russ started to resemble the sweet person he had been as a child.

Because his father (Keith) had also stopped drinking, he and Russ became close for the first time. Jesus Christ mended relationships which human effort could never have healed. Keith came to know the Lord just two days before cancer took his life.

The focus on Bible-based recovery encouraged Bill and me and gave us hope. Although we had known the Lord for years, the Overcomer's Goals helped us keep a balanced perspective. To symbolize our victory in Christ, a family member designed the Overcomer's Cross. (See page one.) This meaningful symbol identifies this Christ-centered approach to recovery.

Overcomers in Christ was too good to keep to ourselves. We had few resources, but God moved His people to help. The Lord's work forged ahead because many gave sacrificially. They shared our passion to meet people at their point of need and lead them to Jesus Christ.

On January 30, 1987, we held the first Overcomers in Christ meeting. The thrill of seeing others recover began to replace the pain of the past. Churches, jails, and missions across the nation welcomed our help in equipping them to lead troubled people to new life in Christ.

The *Overcomer's Handbook* proved effective as a discipling tool regardless of what problems people were struggling with. As the Lord made it possible, we adapted the ministry to meet these widespread needs. Our rapid growth became both a joy and a challenge.

The Lord forged Overcomers in Christ out of our fiery trial. He was preparing us to equip others for Christ-centered recovery. With God's help and the support of His people, we will continue to reach out to those who are hurting. M.L.F.

216   *The Overcomers Story*

BEVERLY V.

Tell us about your life before you found Overcomers in Christ.

I didn't start using until I was in college. I was able to handle my career as a teacher, and later as a social worker, while still drinking. I paid my bills and lived a fairly normal life, but all the while alcoholism was sneaking up on me.

Then about 12 years ago, I moved to a small town. I'd always been a loner, but now I felt more alone and bored than ever. So I drank to get away from my feelings and to get attention.

I got attention all right. I had multiple personalities when I drank. People would say, "Oh no, here she comes again!" I had lots of action with cabs and rescue squads coming and going.

Things got so bad that my family had me referred to the mental health board. I was sent to a treatment center but stayed in total denial. I wouldn't admit I had a problem, so I didn't respond to treatment.

Five years later, I got sent to treatment again. I was finally ready to face my addiction and cooperate. No one expected me to stay straight, but I got over two years sobriety before I had a fall.

Tell us what happened.

I decided to test myself. I'd had oral surgery and was on a prescribed medication. That didn't kill the pain, so I decided to drink two or three beers. I thought maybe I could drink just a couple and not get drunk. But my system was so clean that the alcohol, along with the medication, really did a number on me. I ended up in the hospital for six days.

Then my brother told me about Overcomers in Christ. Although I hadn't been able to find my niche in other support groups, I promised to try the program.

Two days after getting out of the hospital, I went to a meeting and have attended regularly ever since. Overcomers in Christ is one of the best things that ever happened to me.

In what way did Overcomers in Christ change your life?

I found the Lord. I'd known since childhood that Christ died for me. But now I've learned how to apply God's Word *personally*. While reading John 3:16, it dawned on me that because Christ died for my sins, I have eternal life. I found such peace just by believing what God says.

Also the meetings give me the fellowship and support I need. If I'd been in this group, I don't think I would've broken my sobriety.

> "Now I've learned how to apply God's Word *personally*."

Beverly V. 217

> "I think a person can learn from a mistake and go on."

How do you work the program?

I use the Handbook. Though I knew little about the program, I started writing the answers to the Go For The Goals study questions. I feel that writing the Goals helps me absorb them. I'm learning how each Goal fits the others like a piece of a puzzle. The more I work the program, the more it makes sense.

What does recovery mean to you?

It's inner peace through Christ living within me. Before I do things, it's asking myself, "Would Christ do this?" And to me recovery means sharing this wonderful, Christ-centered program with others.

What can you say to someone who has a so-called "slip?"

I planned my fall, so I don't call it a slip. I think a person can learn from a mistake and go on. Anyone who falls should go to meetings and get the help they need. Above all, I'd encourage them to get into the Goals. The Lord has used them to do wonders for me.

Make It Personal

In what way does Beverly's testimony benefit or challenge you?

218   *Beverly V.*

Bob W.

How did you get started in pornography and sexual addiction?

I was sexually abused by female babysitters when I was only five. Then my uncle, who was into pornography, abused me when I was seven. Both my parents used hard-core porn. Mom and Dad both worked and were never home so I grew up watching porn films.

It's little wonder that you got into pornography. Then how did you discover that you were addicted?

I didn't wake up to my addiction until years later when I lost my wife and children. Heartsick, I decided to look into the harmful effects of pornography. I discovered that my shameful behavior followed four steps taken by most porn addicts:

1. *Addiction*—the use of porn became compulsive, consuming my thoughts and time.

2. *Escalation*—To get the same sexual stimulation as before, I required increased lewdness, grossness, or violence.

3. *Desensitization*—what previously was shocking and disturbing became acceptable.

4. *Acting Out*—I began engaging in the sexual activities seen in the pornography.

> "Members made it clear that they didn't change themselves—it was Christ in them that made the difference."

You certainly needed help to break out of that addictive cycle. How has Overcomers in Christ helped you do that?

When I went to my first meeting, I didn't even know what Overcomers in Christ was. A friend said he was going, and I asked if I could go along. I was amazed to find a Christ-centered outreach to help people like me. The group played the Dealing with Feeling® card game and shared with each other. I don't remember the topic of the discussion that followed, but I do know it was exactly what I needed.

I could see Christ in the changed lives of people in the group. Members made it clear that they didn't change themselves—it was Christ in them that made the difference. I wanted that. Since then I've been attending regularly and find that the support and fellowship really help me.

Does this meeting deal specifically with sexual addiction or are people with other addictions involved?

The group I joined deals mostly with drug and alcohol addiction. However, I've found that the Overcomer's Goals apply to my problem too. After studying Goal Twelve, Outreach, I decided to start a group especially for overcoming sex, love, and pornography addiction.

Bob W. 219

FELLOW RUNNERS
Testimonies

Do you feel sexual addiction differs from other compulsive behaviors?

There's more guilt, shame, and denial for the sexual addict than with any other addiction. In most circles, it's not okay to admit you've got this problem.

Do you see a relationship between sexual addiction and drugs and alcohol?

Often people use drugs and alcohol to mask the shame and guilt from sexual sins. It's a vicious cycle because people do things they are ashamed of when they're stoned. Then they sober up and feel guilty and use again to try to get rid of the guilt. But the only way to get rid of guilt is through Christ.

Do you think sexual addiction is a problem in the church?

Definitely. The first thing we've got to do is admit there's a problem. There are pastors and church leaders who have fallen. I was a member of a Bible-believing church while involved in pornography.

Churches need Christ-centered support groups where people can feel free to open up. And pastors must be trained to counsel those with sexual problems.

Confidentiality is extremely important in this type of group. I believe that the time and place of a sexual addiction meeting should remain unpublished.

> "The only way to get rid of guilt is through Christ."

Make It Personal

In what way does Bob's testimony benefit or challenge you?

_____

_____

_____

_____

_____

_____

_____

_____

_____

_____

DeDee C.

Describe your childhood.

I used to take my dad's beer out of the refrigerator and drink to stay out of the way. My father was a practicing alcoholic and my mother was dysfunctional. I didn't have any friends. Daddy was a bookie and usually drunk, so I couldn't bring friends home.

My first child was born when I was 14. I got married, but it wasn't long before I ran away with another guy.

Eventually, I remarried again to a verbally abusive man. That lasted only a year before I took my daughter and left.

Life wasn't going too well for you at this point.

No, and things didn't get any better. About the time I left my second husband, I discovered the bar scene. Everyone accepted me there. Men told me how beautiful I was and that they loved me. I became very promiscuous and wound up in some scary situations.

No one had ever introduced me to the Lord, but I prayed. I'd come home drunk and pray.

I was in and out of relationships with alcoholic men for four years. It was really sick. Then I met Mark and married again. He was alcoholic and from an alcoholic home. But he was exciting! Mark was a good dancer. That's why I married him.

About four years ago, a friend at work invited me to church, and I found the Lord. I was thrilled and tried to tell everyone about Him. However, I didn't deal with my own problems, so I wasn't a very good example of Christianity.

Coming to know the Lord probably gave you some of the love you'd been looking for.

> "I told everybody about my wonderful Lord. But my personal life was still messed up."

It did. I told everybody about my wonderful Lord. But my personal life was still messed up. Mark left me, and I didn't know if I was going to make it.

I turned to stealing and got arrested. It was the best thing that could've happened because it brought me out of denial. It was amazing how I had deceived myself into thinking that God wanted me to have the things I was stealing.

After the arrest, I began three years of therapy. I learned that not everybody steals. Not everybody comes from a drunk family. Not everybody beats you up to show that they love you.

DeDee C. 221

Well, how did you discover Overcomers in Christ?

I went into an arcade and found a brochure about Overcomers. I went to a meeting, and it wasn't anything real big. But I'd had bad experiences with other support groups, so I was expecting disappointment. Then I went again, and it just hit me that the hole in my heart was being filled with God! It was like I "felt" a thought.

I continued attending O.I.C. with that thought in mind and began getting something out of the meetings. Soon, I was so on fire—it was like I had found the Lord all over again! I knew I wanted to start a group in my church.

It seems that many adult children have multiple addictions. What has been your experience?

Most of the people in my group have been into all of the addictions. I think that adult children have multiple addictions because they're searching for identity. I believe God created us all with an inner hole, so we can fill it with Him.

> "I believe God created us all with an inner hole, so we can fill it with Him."

Make It Personal

In what way does DeDee's testimony benefit or challenge you?

_____

_____

_____

_____

_____

_____

_____

_____

_____

_____

_____

_____

DENNIS F.

Let's begin before you got into recovery. What's it like to be a Christian and a practicing drug addict at the same time?

It's like living two different lives. But I didn't think I had a problem, so I didn't allow myself to feel guilty. I even had myself fooled into thinking I was more "spiritual" when I was high.

In reality how did using create problems for you?

As you can imagine, it created difficulty in witnessing for the Lord. I would get high with the guys at work and then try to tell them about the Lord. Since my life wasn't much different than theirs, I didn't get too far.

I did many things I shouldn't have. Several times I told my dad that I needed money to buy groceries, then used it to buy a bag. I worked six and seven days a week to feed my habit, but that still wasn't enough.

I spent a great deal of time getting high when I could have been doing something worthwhile. And I used pot to avoid conflict. If a problem came up, it was easier to get high than deal with it. Also, I had a lot of mood swings. I didn't realize how bad it was until I got into recovery.

So you had a problem, but you just didn't recognize it.

That's right. I focused on my wife's addiction instead of my own. I had tunnel vision and kept so busy trying to help her that I couldn't see my own problem.

What turned you around?

A guy at work got fired for coming to work wasted. That got me thinking. I began feeling tired of the whole empty lifestyle—the Saturday night drives, the working constantly to support my habit, the whole bit. And watching my wife get worse and worse, I felt like one of us had to do something to change.

"I knew it was time to 'get off the pot' and get going!"

As the truth started to dawn on me, I realized I wasn't living a Christ-honoring life. Then a Christian friend encouraged me to get into Overcomers in Christ. She told me that I could help reach others for the Lord if I would just deal with my addiction. I knew it was time to "get off the pot" and get going!

What part has Overcomers in Christ had in your recovery?

The main thing is that I've got somebody to talk to when I'm having a tough time who won't tell everybody what I say. Since I've been in the program almost two years, I know the Goals pretty well. I've learned the hard way that I have to be truthful, that I especially have to watch my attitude, and take care of my health. If I neglect any of the Goals, I'm in danger of relapse.

Dennis F. 223

"The reality is— if it causes you problems, then you've got a problem."

How do you define recovery?

It means staying straight, of course. But it means a whole lot more. It's learning a whole new lifestyle and how to deal with my problems instead of trying to escape by using.

What do you wish to share with others who are in denial like you were?

The reality is—if it causes you problems, then you've got a problem. When you admit you need help, O.I.C. can show you the way to recovery. I know because it worked for me.

Make It Personal

In what way does Dennis's testimony benefit or challenge you?

Ed B.

How has Overcomers in Christ impacted your personal life?

O.I.C. changed my life as it helped me rethink some issues in my life. I became more aware of certain areas in my personal relationship with Christ that were lacking spiritually. I have been involved in rescue ministry for much of my Christian life. O.I.C. showed me that even though I had been doing a good work, I had been doing it in my own strength. In working the program with others, I began relaxing in and relying on my Lord Jesus Christ. My life became easier and more effective.

In what ways do you use our material to help others?

I use Overcomers in Christ materials in a number of ways. My involvement includes support group meetings, prison ministries, aftercare for releasees, family recovery issues, and one on one mentoring. I have found that there have been no barriers of resistance sexually, racially, culturally, or denominationally once they actually look at the material.

How do you qualify a person as being able to benefit from O.I.C.?

"The Dealing with Feeling® card game is fantastic. The game gets men to talk, really talk!"

Everyone has gaps in their understanding of life's problems and issues. I know of no one who could not benefit from Overcomers in Christ. I know this sounds fanatical. It is not. It is just that I know it works. I have seen and am still seeing God use O.I.C. in the lives of diverse individuals: Incarcerated or free, educated or not, rich or poor, men, women, children, teens, as well as those with different cultural backgrounds. It's thrilling to be a part of O.I.C. as God uses the material and our team to work in the lives of people internationally.

What response have you seen from the Dealing with Feeling® communication game?

The Dealing with Feeling® card game is fantastic. The game gets men to talk, really talk! Men, in general, involve themselves in a lot of shallow non-talk. Conversations that do little or nothing to deepen their relationship with God or with other people. How exciting to hear men (and women) discuss their Savior with the same enthusiasm, or more, than their favorite sport.

What do you see as unique to Overcomers in Christ?

The fact that we can discuss current problems in our life in a Christ-centered context. Christ, Lordship, and improving our serve is central to O.I.C. literature. This comes out in every meeting and contact. I participate in several Overcomers in Christ groups. Each group has its own personality, its own approach to applying the 12 Goals in the Handbook. The diversity of the groups is especially helpful in that I don't get a one sided view of spiritual issues. The program is forcefully confrontational, but not in an "in-your-face" offensive way.

Ed B. 225

> *"I know of no one who could not benefit from Overcomers in Christ."*

Can you share an example of how you have seen God work?

Working prayerfully through Goal Two, ATTITUDE, I have repeatedly seen people discover God's grace. They realized that they were trying in their own strength to change the bad attitudes that were producing displeasing actions. They came to understand that they needed to get their inner beliefs in line with the TRUTH (Goal One) then let God's Holy Spirit do the work. Relief and peace came over them as they learned to rest in His grace instead of depending on themselves.

Make It Personal

In what way does Ed's testimony benefit or challenge you?

GLEN C.

As a Christian, why do you need a recovery plan to help you overcome your addiction?

Some people expect those who find Christ to be automatically healed of their addictions. But I've found that, although Christ gives me the power to overcome, I still need to deal with addiction one day at a time.

Tell us a little about your background.

Although I grew up attending a Bible-believing church, I went astray. My mother was a Christian, so I was taught about Jesus from childhood. However, I did not know Him personally. My father was an alcoholic who died of throat cancer when I was in my teens. I became a drug addict and alcoholic myself and was nearly killed before I found the Lord.

How did you get started using alcohol and drugs?

I started drinking heavily the summer between junior and senior high school while staying with relatives. As I was growing up, I noticed that the men always drank at social events. So I had the idea that it was manly to drink.

From alcohol I went to pot, then acid, speed, crank, and other drugs. I had always been shy, and going along with the using crowd made me feel more accepted.

When did you discover that you had a problem?

Even though I did a lot of partying, I didn't think I had a problem. I thought that because I earned the money to support my habit and didn't need to steal, I was okay. It wasn't until I had a nearly fatal accident that I faced reality.

Tell us about it.

I'd been partying for at least 12 hours. I lost my balance and fell 27 feet from a third-story balcony. I struggled to get up but lost consciousness. I woke up in the hospital with a fractured spine, a broken foot, and messed up knees.

I knew Christ had saved me from death and had a purpose for my life. I felt a real need for Him. After 31 days in the hospital, I went to stay with my mom while continuing to recover.

How did you find the Lord and Overcomers in Christ?

After I was well enough to live on my own, I found the Lord through a neighborhood church. The pastor had one-on-one Bible studies with me explaining that Christ died for me. After a few weeks, I accepted the Lord and decided to go all out for Him. That didn't mean that I'd completely overcome my addiction, but it was a beginning.

"It wasn't until I had a nearly fatal accident that I faced reality."

Glen C.

With my pastor's encouragement, I started Bible school. There, a fellow student told me about Overcomers in Christ. Eventually, I was asked to help start a group in our church. I was excited about the opportunity to help others.

How does working with others affect your own recovery?

I no longer feel alone or looked down upon. I can relate to members, and they can relate to me.

Do you think that Bible schools are equipping students to work with the addicted?

No. Students might work with the addicted at a mission or jail. But the addicted are everywhere—even in church. I think Christians need to be taught how to reach the addicted. I see a need for more openness among Christians so that people who need help can get it.

How has Overcomers in Christ changed your life?

Overcomers has given me a sense of belonging and a purpose in life. God has shown me that He can use me to help others find victory through Christ.

> "I see a need for more openness among Christians so that people who need help can get it."

Make It Personal

In what way does Glen's testimony benefit or challenge you?

JILL B.

When did drugs and alcohol begin to affect your family?

When our oldest son, Tom, was in the seventh grade we began to suspect a problem. His attitude changed, and he became very rebellious. We knew that something was wrong, but it took us a few months to figure out what it was.

He was an honor roll student and very capable. But then one day he got caught at school with marijuana. He wouldn't smoke cigarettes because he thought they were harmful, but he bought into the idea that marijuana wouldn't hurt him.

Tom was suspended from school, and we grounded him for a month. He took that well but was soon back to using drugs. He left home at 18 and finished school on his own.

What were your feelings at that time?

Scared. Really scared. And embarrassed to have others know that our son was out of control. Angry that living for Christ had not spared me this pain.

When did you get into codependency treatment?

That was with our second son. He had a learning disability and school became an assault on his self-esteem. When his older brother left home, Don became suicidal and had to be hospitalized.

> "I found out that I could not change others, so I learned to let go and let God."

I was numb. I became very depressed and wondered how God could love me and allow such things to happen.

Don was diagnosed as chemically dependent and needed treatment. To get help for him required that one or both parents go through codependency treatment.

What did you gain through treatment?

I found out that I could not change others, so I learned to "let go and let God". I realized that I couldn't let my sons' problems destroy my serenity and peace with God.

Then how did you hear about Overcomers in Christ?

It was a number of years later through our teenage daughter. There had been a presentation to her youth group at church, and she carried some literature home. She had been experimenting with drugs, so I asked her to go to Overcomers in Christ.

In what way did O.I.C. minister to your needs?

I attended at first because of my daughter. I felt a little uncomfortable because the group met in my home church, and I didn't want to see anyone I knew.

Jill B. 229

But that passed after the first two meetings. I was glad to find a Christ-centered program and people who understood.

Eventually you became a group leader. Why were you willing to make that commitment?

I was very positive about the program and what it could do for families. I felt like what I'd been through prepared me to help others.

Is there anything you would like to share with parents who are trying to cope with a wayward son or daughter?

Love them unconditionally. With a counselor's help, we realized our suicidal son needed strong, verbal communication that he was loved. I think all teens need that.

Also, I think it's important to keep our relationship with the Lord strong. The troubled teen looks to us to see how problems affect our walk with Christ. We shouldn't hide our feelings from them, and we shouldn't panic. Overcomers in Christ helps by supporting us through the tough times.

> "I felt like what I'd been through prepared me to help others."

Make It Personal

In what way does Jill's testimony benefit or challenge you?

230 *Jill B.*

JULIA P.

Can you tell us how you developed an eating disorder?

As a small child, I was sexually abused by a so-called "friend" of the family. With an alcoholic father and a domineering mother, I'm what you call a "textbook" case.

I was only five and had no resources to deal with the pain of sexual abuse. In order to feel better about myself, I tried to do everything I was told. I began overeating to try to find relief. Dieting didn't help, so by the time I was eight, I was put on diet pills.

Describe your teenage and early adult years.

Isolated. My parents were divorced when I was twelve. As a teenager, my free time was spent helping my mother with housework or cooking. I had no social life and avoided men. In college and beyond, I had difficulty relating to others and tried taking my life many times.

I remember one Friday night when I took everything in my medicine cabinet to try to end it all. I slept through till Sunday and woke up with my dog licking my face. I was such a loner that nobody missed me.

How did you begin to get help?

I married a man I met on a blind date. His sister-in-law suspected that I had an eating disorder and gave me a book on the subject. The book helped me recognize my problem, and I went to the doctor. He referred me to a counselor who recommended inpatient treatment.

Wasn't it about that time that you were introduced to Overcomers in Christ?

Yes. A Christian counselor referred me to an Overcomers in Christ eating disorder group. I took an *Overcomer's Handbook* home from the first meeting and started working on the Goals right away. I've felt like a normal person for the first time in my life.

I confessed to my husband that I had an eating disorder—as if he didn't know! Admitting my addiction (and putting a label on it) helped free me.

"You will know the truth, and the truth will set you free" is for real, isn't it?

Literally. When I first began to realize this new freedom, I spent days just being happy. I had begged God to release me. Now that He has, I sometimes feel I can't contain the joy. My Bible is almost dancing. I read it every day expecting to get something, and I do.

> "I took an *Overcomer's Handbook* home from the first meeting and started working on the Goals right away. I've felt like a normal person for the first time in my life."

Julia P. 231

How do you work on the Goals?

At my first meeting, the leaders told me to get a notebook and write, write, write, so that's what I've been doing. I work on one section of a Goal each day by writing out the answers to the Go For The Goals questions. It's been the best thing I could have done to help myself.

Tell us more about how recovery has changed your life.

I have friends now. Since I've joined Overcomers in Christ, I feel like I belong. And I've come to feel at home in church too. For years I served God out of fear. Now, I serve Him because I love Him. A deep, personal relationship with the Lord has filled the hole in my heart.

"A deep, personal relationship with the Lord has filled the hole in my heart."

What effect has leading an O.I.C. group had on your recovery?

Leading a group humbles me and keeps me focused on recovery. It reminds me of where I came from because I see people who are where I was.

I'm amazed how members share their deepest feelings. I've been in support groups before but never in one where we get right down to the problem like we do here.

Make It Personal

In what way does Julia's testimony benefit or challenge you?

_____

_____

_____

_____

_____

_____

_____

_____

_____

_____

_____

LORI W.

Describe your life before Overcomers in Christ.

Crazy. I lived in fear that the police would come to the door telling me my husband was dead. And I allowed my alcoholic, drug-addict husband to make a doormat out of me. He had complete control over the finances, and we were terribly in debt. Our dysfunctional home caused our children to be insecure. Through all this I found little understanding from my Christian friends. They thought Christians weren't supposed to have those kinds of problems.

You drive over 20 miles one way to come to a meeting. What is it that brings you back week after week?

The Christian support and fellowship. I feel that I can open up about my failures without being looked down on. And listening to others helps me see things more clearly. I like it that we can talk about the Lord.

What specific benefits have you received from Overcomers in Christ?

I learned to overcome my codependent habits. Also, I got major help with my overeating. I feel that my addiction was just as severe as my husband's. Food addiction was destroying my relationship with others and my self-esteem.

How much weight have you lost?

Almost 115 pounds. The Lord has helped me to face up to my food addiction and codependency. As I read the Handbook, I focus on my own problems instead of my husband's.

How do you work the program other than attending meetings?

I read the Handbook in the morning along with my Bible. I go through the Goals and apply them to my life.

How has your husband changed since you got involved in O.I.C.?

I've seen an improvement in his attitude. I've learned that I can't change him, but as I change, he tends to respond by changing also.

What can you say to someone whose spouse discourages him or her from coming to O.I.C.?

I think it's vital for a person to get into recovery anyway. Nobody's going to recover until somebody chooses to get well. Otherwise, you keep going around in a vicious circle. I don't think the Lord expects people to let a sick partner dominate them. But I understand those who fall into that trap because I did it myself. I learned later that I was only enabling my husband to continue using.

> "Nobody's going to recover until somebody chooses to get well. Otherwise, you keep going around in a vicious circle."

Lori W. 233

> *"I enjoy encouraging others and usually end up being encouraged myself."*

As someone who's had little support-group experience, how difficult do you find it to lead a meeting?

It's easy. I simply follow the Way To Go* format. And I rely on the Go For The Goals and the Dealing with Feeling® game to help keep the discussion moving. Sometimes we discuss a topic instead of working on a Goal. I enjoy encouraging others and usually end up being encouraged myself.

*The Way To Go suggested format is on the inside back cover.

Make It Personal

In what way does Lori's testimony benefit or challenge you?

_____

_____

_____

_____

_____

_____

_____

_____

_____

_____

_____

_____

_____

_____

Lori W.

MIKE H.

What is your background?

I started using drugs and alcohol at about nine years old and became heavily addicted to both. Constantly under the influence, I was in and out of jail. I accepted Christ about 20 years ago while serving jail time. But I didn't tell anybody. They had no Christian program there, so I didn't grow. When I got out, I got drunk before I even got on the bus. The next 15 years were downhill.

How did you get involved with Overcomers in Christ?

I began going to church because I wanted my son to be brought up right. I publicly expressed my commitment to Jesus Christ. But I still couldn't stay sober. When visiting one church, I filled out a prayer card asking for a Christian A.A. sponsor. One of the elders there told me about the Overcomers program that was about to start. I told him they'd better start it soon because I couldn't stay sober 30 days. On January 30, 1987, I attended the first Overcomers meeting.

After struggling so many years, did you expect to find sobriety?

I was real skeptical and apprehensive. I knew God wanted me to get involved, but I hadn't learned to surrender yet. But I'd reached the end of my rope— I had to go somewhere. So the first night I went to Overcomers, I went under the influence.

> "I keep too busy doing the right things to find time to get into trouble."

How do you explain the fact that you found victory while some people attend meetings but stay in bondage?

Commitment and true surrender. A couple of days after my first meeting, I was playing horseshoes and drinking as usual. I poured out a beer on the ground and said, "God, this Bud's for you. I did my part, now you do yours." Then, I started getting into the program. I looked into the Handbook and started devouring it.

It was commitment to Christ and the program that did it. I go to Him every day. I think what happens is that people try to go from week to week and from meeting to meeting. In the beginning, I went from hour to hour.

For example, when I'd go to the grocery store, there were certain aisles the cart would almost go to by itself. Well, I'm a graphic person. So I'd say out loud, "Get back, Satan! Jesus, you'd better get him out of here." Of course, I got some strange looks, but I had lots of room in the aisles. Now I'm not saying everybody should do that, but it worked for me.

Like I told you, I really got into the program. I think some people have one foot in and one foot out.

Mike H. 235

So you used the program to renew your mind every single day?

Every day. I should know the Overcomer's Prayer by heart, but I purposely put up a mental block so I have to open my Handbook and read it every day. And I keep the Handbook in my Bible case so I have to open my Bible. All that's done during my quiet time.

Do you have any other tips for people who are struggling?

Yes. It's important to get into a group where people will pray for you regularly. I know God understands our grunts and groans, but it's good to get into a group of people who know how to pray.

Another thing that really helps me is keeping busy every night with Overcomers meetings, church, fellowship, and other Christ-related activities (except for one family night). I keep too busy doing the right things to find time to get into trouble.

Why do you attend the meetings so regularly?

More than anything else, it's fellowship. Sometimes I need the meeting, and sometimes the meeting needs me. And it's a way to reach out to others. I'm learning to let God love others through me.

> "Sometimes I need the meeting, and sometimes the meeting needs me."

Make It Personal

In what way does Mike's testimony benefit or challenge you?

_____

_____

_____

_____

_____

_____

_____

_____

_____

_____

_____

_____

PAT B.

Share a little of your background with us.

I had an alcoholic father and was married three times, twice to alcoholics. I married to get away from home and fill the emptiness in my life. After a year and a half with my first husband, I split. My solution to problems was to run away.

Immediately, I began looking for another husband and married again to a very nice man who belonged to a cult. Years later, when I finally got out of the cult, we no longer had anything in common. I left husband number two and started looking for another. I just could not be alone.

Soon I met Al. I thought the way he reacted to me was love. ("I can't live without you, I must have you," etc.) I thought that was wonderful. At last maybe I'd found someone who loved me. Al worked at a drug rehab center and was on parole. He worked with drug addicts all week, then drank all weekend. It was crazy.

Now I had the idea that if you help people get what they want out of life, they'll discontinue destructive, insane behavior. (WRONG!) So I helped Al go back to college and get his degree. He was very smart and got his undergraduate and masters degrees in social work. He was drinking and gambling all the way through school.

"Overcomers expands my relationship with Jesus into many areas of life..."

Then, he had an affair, and I filed for divorce. But I still felt responsible for him. I sold my property to pay his school bills and other debts. I also helped Al finish his master's thesis. I was on an emotional roller coaster and began searching desperately for another man.

How did you break this unhealthy cycle?

For me it was finding the Lord and getting into recovery. I evaluated my life and saw that I was going nowhere. So I started attending a nearby church. I cried all through the service saying, "God, if there is a God, I need help." Several months later I accepted Christ as my Savior.

You finally found someone to love you unconditionally.

Yes, I'd been looking for the Lord all along.

My life began to change, but I was still hanging on to Al. Even knowing the Lord didn't break the emotional ties to my ex-husband, and I started thinking about suicide. My girlfriend called a local treatment center, and I went in for codependency treatment. There I discovered that I had not dealt with the pain of my childhood even though my father and I had become good friends. By dealing with my past and getting in touch with my feelings, I found a wonderful, new freedom.

Pat B. 237

How did you get started with Overcomers in Christ?

My pastor told me about it and loaned me a Handbook. I went "WOW!" because when I was in other support groups, I'd wanted to share that the only answer was Jesus Christ. But that was a no-no. So I was thrilled to find a Christ-centered program.

What do you especially like about Overcomers in Christ?

Anybody, whether codependent or not, can use the Overcomer's Goals. The Goals have taken me deeper into God's Word. They contain priceless secrets that could only have come from the Lord.

Another thing I like is the beautiful simplicity of the program. At one time my life was so complicated that I got headaches trying to figure out the right decisions. Now when I start to "figure, figure, figure," I turn to the Goals.

What keeps you coming to the meeting?

I learn from others and they learn from me because we understand each other. I don't need to spend hours explaining viewpoints that come from my experience. Overcomers expands my relationship with Jesus into many areas of life and replaces my frustration with victory.

> "The Goals have taken me deeper into God's Word. They contain priceless secrets that could only have come from the Lord."

Make It Personal

In what way does Pat's testimony benefit or challenge you?

_____

_____

_____

_____

_____

_____

_____

_____

_____

_____

_____

_____

_____

TAMMY J.

What is your background?

My birth father abandoned me at an early age. I was also sexually abused as a child. I developed an eating disorder, drug and alcohol problem, and became depressed and codependent. Every area of my life was a mess.

I moved in with my alcoholic boyfriend and eventually married him. I was pregnant and started thinking about how to give our child a better life. I wanted to change but didn't know how.

How did you get into recovery?

After our son was born, we went to live with my husband's relatives. My sister-in-law invited me to go with her to an Overcomers support group.

Share your first impression of Overcomers in Christ.

For the first meeting or two, I just sat in the corner and didn't say a word. But with all the love and acceptance there, I gradually began to open up. I thought the people were nuts, but I knew they had an inner peace that I didn't have. After a few months, our support group leader was able to lead me to the Lord. I felt a relief that I never had before!

Praise the Lord! What happened then?

> "One thing that helped me get a foothold on recovery was going through the Steps to Freedom. I experienced a tremendous healing from anger and unforgiveness."

God had a lot of work to do because my life was in shambles. One thing that helped me get a foothold on recovery was going through the Steps to Freedom.* I experienced tremendous healing from anger and unforgiveness. Finally, I was free to grow and become the person God created me to be.
*See pages 45-96.

How has your recovery affected your husband and children?

The Lord has given me the desire to become a godly wife and mother. I am no longer so absorbed with my own problems that I can't properly care for our children. I am much less likely to yell at our children or emotionally abuse them. My husband has also come to know the Lord. He attends Overcomers in Christ and has begun to deal with his own issues.

In what way has God used your special needs child to motivate you?

God used the difficulty of meeting our son's needs to motivate us to get help. As a parent of a special needs child, I know that our whole family has special needs. God used Overcomers in Christ to help us come to terms with our son's problems. As we let Him work with us, we overcome our own dysfunctional upbringing. We are learning how to be a godly father and mother.

Tammy J. 239

The Lord has enabled you to kick a nicotine addiction that began when you were only five. Tell us how you're finding victory.

After I lost my Mom, I came to realize that I was giving her God's place in my life. Once I gave God His place, I learned to trust Him. I realized that He wanted to be my best friend, so I'm no longer afraid to take a leap of faith. I read my Bible, attend a Bible study, and keep in touch with my prayer partners. And I keep my hands busy. I pray constantly and tell God that He'll have to do it because I can't. For Him, and for my children, I don't give myself any choice but to quit.

What do you get out of your Overcomers support group?

I no longer feel so alone. The support helps me deal with the ups and downs of life, especially the trials with our special needs child. It means so much to have people who accept and understand me and who also hold me accountable. My group helps me to keep growing in the Lord. Also, I enjoy being there to help others. Like the Bible says, we comfort others with the comfort we have received from God.

> "It means so much to have people who accept and understand me and who also hold me accountable."

Make It Personal

In what way does Tammy's testimony benefit or challenge you?

"VALORIE"

What originally brought you to Overcomers in Christ?

I was very confused about social interaction. I tended to pull away and not get very close to people. I wanted to make friends, but I didn't know how and everything I tried didn't work.

How would you describe your childhood?

There was no alcohol, no physical violence, no sexual abuse, nothing like that. There wasn't even any tobacco in the house. But I was very isolated. My parents socialized a lot but left us home with baby-sitters. Mom and Dad's expectations of me were unrealistic. Basically, they expected perfection. As the only daughter, I got lots of responsibility with no authority or credit. I was expected to clean up after my brothers all the time. Anything that went wrong while our parents were gone was seen as my fault. It was extremely emotionally abusive.

How has involvement with Overcomers in Christ changed your life?

It has helped me to see myself as being valuable apart from what I do. I no longer feel I need to be perfect or able to control the outcome of everything. Overcomers in Christ has taught me that truth is my friend, not my enemy. Lies are the enemy. It helped me identify and cling to the truth. I learned to accept that I'm not perfect. When I make a mistake, I don't suddenly belong in a gutter or trash heap.

How do you explain this turn around?

I came to realize that there are lies in the way I think about myself, the way I see the world, and the way I see God. Now I've made it my life goal to replace those lies with God's truth. So when I get uncomfortable, I ask myself, "What is the truth in this situation?"

In what way has your understanding of who God is changed?

I used to see God as a perfectionist. Now I see that God's into the motive of the heart and into character. It's okay if I fail as long as I'm trying. I've come to understand that God isn't as interested in where I am as where I'm going and why.

How has your ability to relate to others changed?

I feel less like I'm stupid and different from everyone else. Overcomers in Christ has helped me take other people off a pedestal and meet them at eye level. I have learned to give people the benefit of the doubt and not automatically judge actions. I am more understanding and view others from a positive rather than negative viewpoint.

> "I no longer feel that I need to be perfect or able to control the outcome of everything."

What keeps you coming to the group?

Fellowship. The feeling that I belong and have common ground. We relate in group in a way that I can't relate to most other people. Pain is a common bond, even though it's not the same pain. People are encouraged to express their hurt rather than hide their problems.

"When I get to Overcomers... I feel that it's okay to be me."

How does your support group help equip you for growth?

It gives me an outlet. Generally when I'm in group situations elsewhere, it's uncomfortable. But when I get to Overcomers, I no longer feel trapped. I feel that it's okay to be me. Nobody is going to discard me or walk away like I've just dumped the whole world on their shoulders. I also feel like I've got something to offer. I've been through some experiences that can help somebody else.

Make It Personal

In what way does Valorie's testimony benefit or challenge you?

_____

_____

_____

_____

_____

_____

_____

_____

_____

_____

_____

Section Eight

TEAMS IN TRAINING
Support Group Know-How

Those who hope in the Lord

will soar like eagles. Isaiah 40:31

- Support Group Guidelines
- Support Group Overview
- Servant-Leaders
- Getting Started
- Meeting How To
- Frequently Asked Questions
- Institutional Groups
- The Overcomer's Prayer

SUPPORT GROUP GUIDELINES

Most group problems come from ignoring one or more of these Guidelines.

1. **PURPOSE**—We meet regularly to share the strength, hope and comfort found in Jesus Christ. Through His unconditional love and victory at the cross, we find the strength to overcome. **"Praise... the God of all comfort, who comforts us in all our troubles, so that we can comfort those in any trouble with the comfort we ourselves have received from God."** (2 Corinthians 1:3-4)

2. **FOCUS**—We find freedom as we become Christ-centered rather than self-centered. Instead of struggling to forgive ourselves, we accept His forgiveness. Rather than working to make ourselves good, we receive His goodness. Instead of trying hard to accept ourselves, we find acceptance in Him. **"This is love; not that we loved God, but that He loved us and sent His Son as a sacrifice for our sins."** (1 John 4:10)

3. **MEMBERSHIP**—We welcome teens and adults who desire a safe place to heal and grow in Christ. To encourage deep sharing and avoid unhealthy relationships, we offer separate groups for males and females. Fellowship with one another helps us more effectively resist Satan and obey God's loving command: **"Do not be overcome by evil, but overcome evil with good."** (Romans 12:21)

4. **AUTHORITY**—We regard the Bible as our "owner's manual" for life. Therefore, any teaching which does not agree with God's Word is unacceptable. We focus on the *practical application* of the Scriptures in our Handbook or other study material. (In-depth Bible study is done outside of group time.) **"God has given us great and precious promises, so that through them [we] may...escape the corruption caused by evil desires."** (2 Peter 1:4)

5. **RESPONSIBILITY**—We accept personal responsibility to live in the light of God's truth. We encourage one another to walk with God by setting a good example. However, we do not control one another's recovery or try to force anyone to change. Instead, we let God's Word and our example speak for itself. **"Be completely humble and gentle; be patient, bearing with one another in love."** (Ephesians 4:2)

6. **ACCOUNTABILITY**—We understand that our group and servant-leaders are accountable to our sponsoring ministry. However, we solve our problems within the group whenever possible. Individually, we may hold ourselves accountable to a sponsor-mentor who serves as a role model. **"Follow my example, as I follow the example of Christ."** (1 Corinthians 11:1)

7. **SHARING**—We give everyone the opportunity to share their feelings, thoughts, and experiences. We listen to each other with respect and direct our conversation to the entire group. No one may dominate the discussion with detailed explanations or become the focal point of the

entire meeting. Also, offensive language is not appropriate or acceptable. To provide a safe place to share, what is said in the meeting stays there. **"A gossip betrays a confidence, but a trustworthy person keeps a secret."** (Proverbs 11:13)

8. **UNITY**—We **"accept one another as Christ has accepted [us]."** Group unity and welfare come before personal interests. Therefore, no one may disrupt a meeting. To avoid controversy, we express opinions only on issues related to recovery in Christ. We refuse to discuss or practice denominational distinctives during group (tongues, baptism, etc.). We **"make every effort to keep the unity of the Spirit through the bond of peace."** (Romans 15:7; Ephesians 4:3)

9. **PRAYER**—We take one another's needs to God because we know that He answers prayer. Exchanging prayer requests and answers encourages us to pray for each other during the week. **"Confess your sins to each other and pray for each other so that you may be healed."** (James 5:16)

> Face your problems with quietness, love, and prayer, and you'll find victory every time.
> Charles Stanley

10. **ANONYMITY**—We have the option to remain anonymous to avoid drawing attention to ourselves. In our meetings, we use first names only. **"[Jesus] must increase, but [we] must become less."** (John 3:30)

11. **HEALTH**—We promote good health by not smoking during our meetings. If we serve beverages containing caffeine, we offer a healthful alternative. **"Do you not know that your body is the temple of the Holy Spirit?"** (1 Corinthians 6:19)

12. **OFFERINGS**—We realize that others have given so that we can be offered recovery without charge. Therefore, at each meeting, we receive $1.00 or more from everyone who can give. In addition to supporting our home church, we send love gifts to Overcomers in Christ whenever possible. **"Freely you have received, freely give."** (Matthew 10:8)

Group Evaluation

Occasionally your group may wish to do an evaluation as to how well you are following the Group Guidelines. Also, ask members the following questions:

a. How do you benefit from this group?

b. In what ways do you contribute to this group?

c. What changes do you feel would increase group effectiveness?

d. What are you doing to interact with members outside of group time?

Support Group Guidelines 245

SUPPORT GROUP OVERVIEW

Ever since Adam and Eve sinned, mankind has needed recovery to God and one another.

1. **Why not just use the Bible instead of a recovery program?**

   Recovery requires interaction with role models and encouragers. The Scriptures acknowledge our need for help to apply biblical truth to our lives. A man reading the Bible was asked, **"Do you understand what you are reading?"** He replied, **"How can I, unless someone explains it to me?"*** A biblical recovery program provides practical guidance and support for overcoming life controlling problems.
   *Acts 8:30-31

2. **Does *everyone* need recovery?**

   Our relationship with God and others indicates our need for recovery. Luke 10:27 sets the standard for healthy living. **"Love the Lord your God with all your heart, and with all your soul, and with all your strength, and with all your mind; and love your neighbor as yourself."** To the extent that we fall short of this, we need recovery. Ever since Adam and Eve sinned, mankind has needed recovery to God and one another. (See the definition of recovery on page 203.)

3. **To whom is Overcomers in Christ material helpful?**

   Teens and adults, whether male or female, unchurched or churched, unsaved or saved, uneducated or educated. We thank the Lord for testimonies of changed lives from people in all walks of life!

4. **Do you recommend separate groups for men and women?**

   Yes. People in recovery are particularly vulnerable to unhealthy relationships. Therefore, we recommend separate groups for men and women. Also, people will usually share more openly without the distraction of the opposite sex.

5. **What is the biblical perspective on small groups?**

   The Lord Jesus spent more time with the Twelve than with the masses. He frequently ministered to small groups in homes. Support groups help Christians follow our Lord's example. Many Bible teachings, such as making disciples or bearing one another's burdens, would be impossible without small-group interaction.

6. **What is an Overcomers in Christ support group?**
   A support group is a small group of people who meet regularly to share the strength and comfort found in Christ. Support groups normally meet on an ongoing basis and remain open to newcomers. Members encourage one another in Christ-centered recovery. The group also provides a safe place to share feelings and prayer requests.

"Overcomers in Christ does not add the Bible to a program but is the program in the Bible."
Wright Proctor

NOTE: A support group is *not* a church substitute, Bible study or group counseling.

7. **Why support groups?**

They provide an effective tool for helping one another apply spiritual truths in a practical way. The biblical command to love, support, and encourage others can readily be fulfilled in a small group. Also, support groups provide the opportunity to be "real" with one another. Christians can put their arms around wounded people through fellowship in a Christ-centered support group.

8. **Why Christ-centered support groups?**

To treat life controlling problems without Christ is like treating cancer with aspirin! You might remove the symptoms, but the problem remains untouched. Without Christ, we have nothing to replace negative habits. Apart from Him, we end up with wasted lives at best and a lost eternity at worst.

Also, Christ-centered recovery overcomes self-centeredness. Instead of using Christ to accomplish our purposes, we let Him use us to accomplish His purposes. Therefore, God's Word forms a vital part of each Overcomers Goal.

9. **What difference does it make whether we identify Jesus Christ as our Higher Power?**

Jesus said, **"Whoever confesses me before men, him will I confess also before my Father who is in heaven. But whoever shall deny me before men, him will I also deny before my Father, who is in heaven." "Whoever shall confess me before men, him shall the Son of Man also confess before the angels of God. But he who denies me before men shall be denied before the angels of God."** Matthew 10:32-33; Luke 12:8-9

These Scriptures have to do with the complete denial of Christ's claim upon our lives. Yet we believe they clearly indicate that we should not be ashamed to identify Jesus Christ as our Higher Power.

10. **How do support groups help build the church?**

Hurting people find help to overcome problems. As they grow spiritually, people become active church members instead of spectators. The Lord receives honor as the church grows in spiritual health and numbers. Pastors and other counselors get better results with less effort. (Please refer to the illustration on page 267.)

11. **How does a support group differ from a Bible study?**

During support group, members focus on the practical application of the Scriptures in their Handbook. Occasionally, they may bring up additional Scriptures. However, to encourage sharing, in-depth Bible study is done outside of group. See page 43 for how to use the Handbook in a Bible study or Sunday school setting.

> To treat life controlling problems without Christ is like treating cancer with aspirin! You might remove the symptoms, but the problem remains untouched.

> Bible study without application is unbiblical.

Support Gruop Overview 247

12. **How does a growth group differ from a support group?**

A growth group meets for in-depth, Christ-centered study for a specific number of weeks. Participation in a growth group requires commitment to do the study and be accountable to others. Until each study is completed, growth groups are closed to newcomers. The unchanging membership allows people to bond and build trust more deeply than might otherwise occur.

13. **What is the relationship between a support group and its sponsoring ministry?**

A sponsoring ministry provides encouragement, public awareness, prayer support, and accountability for the support group. The sponsoring ministry usually supplies the meeting place and may provide other group needs as well. For example, they may stock Handbooks for members. (Except for those having no income, we recommend that people contribute toward their Handbook.) Also, the sponsoring ministry meets with the servant-leaders occasionally for a group progress report. By appointing servant-leaders in whom they have confidence, the sponsoring ministry can respect the group's need for confidentiality.

> By appointing servant-leaders in whom they have confidence, the sponsoring ministry can respect the group's need for confidentiality.

14. **Can a support group be registered without a sponsoring ministry?**

Actually, the *sponsoring ministry* registers with Overcomers in Christ rather than each support group. Being linked to a registered sponsoring ministry enhances the effectiveness of the support group.

The sponsoring ministry provides referrals, prayer, accountability, and guidance. The O.I.C. team can help meet some of these needs, but we recommend that groups hold themselves accountable to their sponsoring ministry.

NOTE: For additional information see, "Getting Started," pages 253-254.

15. **What common problems face a support group ministry?**

- Denial. People often hide behind a religious front to avoid dealing with their problems. Attending church or keeping rules cannot be substituted for a personal relationship with the Lord.
- Wrong teaching. Becoming a Christian doesn't automatically bring victory over life controlling problems. In reality, few people experience instant healing. Instead, we need to learn how to claim victory through Christ on a daily basis.
- A disinterested or judgmental sponsoring ministry. (Group servant-leaders need both accountability and encouragement.)
- Unqualified group leaders. (See servant-leader qualifications on page 249, question #5.)

> Success comes in cans; failure comes in can'ts.

248 *Overview*

SERVANT-LEADERS

Maintaining your own recovery is the "not so secret" secret to successful group leadership.

1. **What are servant-leaders?**

   Servant-leaders are ordinary people through whom God does extraordinary things. They help the members fulfill the purpose for which the group exists.

2. **How are servant-leaders chosen?**

   They are selected by the sponsoring ministry. For the protection of the ministry and the group, volunteers should be chosen prayerfully. The applicant should fill out an application and provide the names of at least three godly people who would recommend them as group leaders. If a group is open to teens, extra caution must be taken when choosing leaders. To be effective, servant-leaders must have the confidence of both the sponsoring ministry and their group.

3. **How many servant-leaders does each group need?**

   At least two. **"Two are better than one, because they have [better results] from their work; if one falls down, his friend can help him up."** (Ecc. 4:9-10) Also, having two servant-leaders makes them more available to the group and helps avoid burnout.

4. **What are the benefits of being a support group servant-leader?**

   Servant-leadership:

   - Helps us become healthier as we work toward our Overcomer's Goals.
   - Encourages us to be "real" with ourselves and others.
   - Increases our ability to effectively minister to hurting people.
   - Teaches us how to relate to people from all walks of life.
   - Provides a way to reach others for our Lord Jesus Christ.
   - Gives us a sense of fulfillment as a channel through whom God works.

Jesus' messages were 30% information and 70% application.

5. **What are the qualifications for servant-leaders?**

   A servant-leader needs to be of the same sex as the group and meet these qualifications:

   - Mature, born again Christian with at least two years in recovery
   - Active member in good standing of a Bible-believing church
   - Agreement with the Overcomers in Christ Statement of Faith (on pages 206-207 under "Choosing A Church Family")
   - Self-worth based on identity in Christ rather than performance or the approval of others
   - Warm, outgoing personality
   - Willing to give at least a six month to one year commitment

Servant-Leaders 249

In addition, successful group leaders are F-A-T.

- F—Faithful (to the Lord and their group)
- A—Available (willing to devote several hours weekly)
- T—Teachable (humble, open to instruction)

> **God works through those of us who realize our weakness. If we think we can handle it, He will let us.**

6. **Can a husband and wife team lead a group?**

If they have a good working relationship, a husband and wife team can lead a support group. However, having a member of the opposite sex as co-leader can inhibit sharing. Also, the likelihood of both servant-leaders being unavailable becomes greater. A better alternative is that the husband help lead a men's group and the wife help lead a women's group.

7. **For what period of time do servant-leaders serve?**

Usually, six months to one year. At the discretion of the sponsoring ministry, they may serve indefinitely.

8. **What training do you recommend for servant-leaders?**

- Read this Handbook from cover to cover. Pay special attention to "Group Guidelines" on pages 244-45 because most group problems result from ignoring them. Also, the "Way To Go" suggested format (inside back cover) will be especially helpful.
- Begin doing "Go For The Goals" (pages 97-200). Servant-leaders should keep themselves *at least* one lesson ahead of the group. (We cannot lead where we have not been.)
- Play Dealing with Feeling® with family and friends. The game will help servant-leaders become more comfortable with in-depth sharing. They should practice reflecting back what is shared. For example, "What I hear you saying is..." or "You feel that..."
- The "Recommended Resources" on pages 210-212 will provide additional insight. Also, see the Overcomers in Christ order form for other resources.

> **Experience is about the cheapest thing we can get if we're wise enough to get it second hand.**

Our material is self-explanatory and user friendly. However, nothing takes the place of practical experience. Therefore, we encourage servant-leaders to keep in contact with us. Our Field Consultant can share how other groups have handled similar issues. It may also be helpful to network with other Christ-centered groups.

9. **To whom are servant-leaders accountable?**

Servant-leaders are accountable to their sponsoring ministry, one another, their group and, above all, to the Lord. (Care must be taken by the sponsoring ministry to respect the confidentiality of the group members.)

10. **What are common pitfalls for servant-leaders to avoid?**

- Failing to apply the Overcomer's Goals to their own lives
- Taking responsibility for others' recovery
- Becoming dependent on the group for approval and acceptance
- Leading from an "I have all the answers" perspective
- Bringing denominational differences into the group
- Turning the meeting into an in-depth Bible study instead of allowing time for sharing

11. **How can servant-leaders keep from dominating the group?**

The Holy Spirit will be active at each meeting, so servant-leaders should expect to learn as well as lead. Rather than doing most of the talking, they should encourage members to express their viewpoint on the material being discussed. Using the Dealing with Feeling® game and the "Go For The Goals" on pages 97-200 will encourage group participation.

12. **What commitment is required of servant-leaders?**

Servant-leaders make at least a six month commitment to:

- Attend the group regularly.
- Help the group fulfill the purpose for which it was established. (One servant-leader serves as the chairperson, the other as the secretary-treasurer. See 13 and 14 below.)
- Hold themselves accountable to their sponsoring ministry.

13. **What are the chairperson's duties?**

The chairperson and secretary-treasurer can decide between them who handles which responsibilities. However, the chairperson usually plans the meetings, choosing the discussion leader or speaker. (S)he opens and closes the meetings and introduces the discussion leader or speaker. (S)he helps keep discussions on track and makes sure that everyone has an opportunity to participate. (S)he also keeps the sponsoring ministry informed of any "Where & When" changes.

14. **What are the secretary-treasurer's duties?**

The secretary-treasurer usually makes announcements and maintains an up-to-date file of member registration cards. After passing the offering box, (s)he records the donations. (S)he pays group expenses, as authorized by the advisory committee,* and sends love offerings to the sponsoring ministry and Overcomers in Christ. Periodically, (s)he checks supplies on hand against a current order form to make sure the group has the necessary supplies. The secretary-treasurer keeps group records, including a copy of the income and expense reports.
*See number 15 on the following page.

> The Holy Spirit will be active at each meeting so servant-leaders should expect to learn as well as lead.

> Don't be afraid to go out on a limb. That's where the fruit is.

Servant-Leaders 251

15. **Who serves on the advisory committee, and what are their duties?**

The advisory committee is made up of the servant-leaders and one or two representatives from the sponsoring ministry (such as a small group coordinator, program director, etc.).

The advisory committee sees that the Group Guidelines are followed. (See pages 244-245.) They also determine how group funds are spent. Using Overcomers in Christ as an information resource, they set policy and solve problems regarding group function.

16. **How can servant-leaders avoid burnout?**

By serving from the overflow of their walk with the Lord. To avoid burnout, quiet time with Him must come before service. Servant-leaders must realize that recovery is the Lord's work. They cannot take responsibility for others' progress. Also, sharing responsibilities and prayer concerns with a co-leader lightens the burden. Keeping in touch with both the sponsoring ministry and Overcomers in Christ encourages and strengthens servant-leaders.

17. **What can be done about servant-leaders who frequently miss meetings?**

Servant-leadership comes from those who can and will attend regularly. That takes commitment and freedom from conflicting responsibilities. Except in unusual circumstances, we suggest that a person automatically forfeits the role of servant-leader by missing three consecutive meetings. However, the sponsoring ministry must make the final decision.

Don't do your bit— do your best.

Notes

GETTING STARTED

> Support groups can best be led by those with at least two years in Christ-centered recovery.

1. **How can a ministry sponsor an Overcomers in Christ support group?**

   • **Choose servant-leaders.** Support groups can best be led by those with at least two years in Christ-centered recovery. Choose two dependable people willing to work on the Overcomer's Goals in their own lives. Leaders need to be of the same sex as the group. (See pages 249-252 for further details.)

   • **Order Supplies.** You will need a Recovery Kit for each servant leader and a Handbook for each group member. Other helpful resources are listed on our order form and web site.

   • **Provide a meeting place.** Invite the group(s) to meet in the ministry facility. Each group needs a room which will accomodate about twelve people. (Station someone at the door to direct newcomers.)

   • **Provide prayer support and accountability.** Pray regularly that the Lord will work through your group. Meet at least quarterly with the servant-leaders for a progress report. Appoint a Small Group Coordinator to provide encouragement for the servant-leaders. A Group Coordinator can also help maintain the balance between confidentiality and accountability.

   • **Register as our Companion Ministry.** We encourage ministries using our materials to register so we can include them in our directory and network more effectively. However, each support group remains accountable to its sponsoring ministry.

   • **Support the ministry.** Please prayerfully consider supporting Overcomers in Christ Ministries as a home mission. Your support enables us to continue to serve the needs of hurting people and to equip our Companion Ministries to do the same.

> "Be strong and courageous. Do not be discouraged, for the Lord your God will be with you wherever you go."
> Joshua 1:9

2. **Do you recommend holding the meeting in someone's home?**

   Many groups have found it better to meet on neutral ground. Home meetings can encourage social visiting rather than getting down to business. Also, problems with privacy arise with members of the household. The sponsoring ministry can either provide or help locate a suitable meeting place.

3. **What are the benefits of registering with Overcomers in Christ?**

   Registration facilitates networking and service. Registered ministries will be included in our Directory and will receive information updates. Registration also qualifies a ministry to apply for a limited license to photocopy for ministry *to street people and the institutionalized.*

Getting Started 253

> Registration facilitates networking and service.

4. **How can we register our group?**

Request a registration form from Overcomers in Christ to be filled out by the sponsoring ministry. Because support groups may multiply or experience other changes, we register the sponsoring ministry rather than each group. There is no charge to register, and the simple form only takes a few moments to complete.

5. **How can we get the word out about our group?**

Spread the word through brochures, flyers, posters, ads, public service announcements, word of mouth, etc. Leave a few brochures with Christians in the helping professions—pastors, counselors, physicians, corrections officers, etc.

You could also hold a public awareness meeting. If the hard-core drug addict and alcoholic are your primary target, show the *Forged In Fire* video (available from Overcomers in Christ). Inquire about other videos to reach the general public. Include personal testimonies from people who've found one-day-at-a-time victory. And don't neglect to share how Overcomers in Christ has benefited you.

6. **How can we avoid being confused with others who use the Overcomers name?**

Use the complete name Overcomers in Christ when explaining who you are. Also, don't refer to the Overcomer's Goals as the Twelve Steps. (However, penal authorities may identify better with the term, Twelve Steps.) And point out the Overcomer's Cross which identifies all Overcomers in Christ material.

> We encourage the sponsoring ministry to maintain a supply of Handbooks so that people can get them immediately.

7. **What supplies do we need to start a group?**

Above all, you need a Recovery Kit for each servant-leader and a Handbook for each member. See our order form for other helpful items.

8. **How can we obtain supplies?**

You can order your supplies directly from Overcomers in Christ. We recommend that the sponsoring ministry maintain a supply of Handbooks so that people can get them immediately. Because people usually do not value what they get for nothing, Handbooks should be given in exchange for an appropriate donation.

9. **What about photocopying the "Go For The Goals" so all members will have a copy?**

Members should be encouraged to obtain their own Handbook. It is illegal to photocopy without written permission. However, registered ministries who sponsor *institutional programs or outreach to street people* may request information about a license to photocopy.

254 *Getting Started*

MEETING HOW TO

> You've never really lived until you've done something for somebody who can never repay you.

1. **What setup do you recommend for a meeting?**

   Many groups like the convenience of sitting around a table. Or set the chairs in a circle (for a feeling of togetherness), and use a side table for the following:

   - Several group copies of the Handbook (clearly marked so they won't get lost or stolen)
   - Dealing with Feeling® communication game
   - Prayer request note pad
   - Caring Connection phone number pad
   - Group offering box

   Put refreshments close by where they can be enjoyed before, during, and after the meeting. Set up a literature table in a visible place where people can get brochures and order Handbooks and other supplies.

   NOTE: We've noticed that a few groups store refreshment supplies and literature in the same box. This practice results in damaged literature.

2. **Why read the Welcome if no newcomers are present?**

   Making the newcomer feel at home is only one of the reasons for reading the Welcome (page 8). It also helps focus on the purpose for the meeting. And it gives a much needed reminder that members are not there to fix one another. In short, the Welcome helps get the meeting started right.

3. **How do you recommend doing self-introductions?**

   We suggest using first names along with sharing what brings you to the group. For example, "I'm Joe. I'm struggling with an alcohol addiction," or "I'm overcoming codependency." Or, "I'm here because I need a safe place to share." Newcomers can simply identify themselves as visitors.

   Awkward situations could arise in a co-ed group when admitting sexual problems. That's another good reason for having separate groups for men and women.

4. **Why is it necessary to avoid denominational issues in support group?**

   Avoiding denominational differences (such as baptism or speaking in tongues) allows your group to reach more people. The Handbook will help you lead participants into spiritual growth without getting sidetracked by denominational issues. *The main thing is to keep the main thing as the main thing!*

> The main thing is to keep the main thing as the main thing!

Meeting How To 255

> Cooperation is spelled with two letters: we.
> G.M. Verity

5. **How can servant-leaders encourage others to share group responsibility such as leading the discussion?**

People are more willing to lead the discussion when they know how easy it is. If they are successfully working toward the Overcomer's Goals, they can lead the discussion. Show them how simple it is to use the "Go For The Goals" as a leader's guide. Assure them that you will be there to help as needed.

As for other miscellaneous responsibilities, ask for a volunteer. People usually respond best when personally asked to do a specific task.

6. **Why not hold longer meetings?**

A longer meeting might be okay occasionally. But we suggest that regular meetings last an hour or hour and a half because:

- Shorter meetings leave time for after-meeting fellowship. (This building of relationships is vital.)
- Most people can only take in about an hour's material at one sitting.
- More people can attend a shorter meeting. (Some have children or other pressing responsibilities.)

7. **If parents can't find a babysitter, what about letting them bring children to group?**

Having young children at a meeting will distract members and inhibit sharing. Also, children could be upset by the emotional intensity that could occur. (However, teens are welcome in O.I.C. groups.) In some groups, the sponsoring ministry provides a volunteer to care for the children. Others use group funds to hire someone.

Children are often as wounded as their parents or more so. They need positive nurturing to break the cycle of dysfunction. Christian bookstores can help locate material for children. Also, contact Confident Kids* for information.
*P.O. Box 11095, Whittier, CA 90603

> Use the Dealing with Feeling® communication game often. It gets beneath the facade and helps remove the mask of denial.

8. **Some members discuss the Goals as if they apply to everyone but themselves. How can they be helped to face reality?**

Remind people to focus on their own recovery. When sharing, members speak in terms of "I" rather than "you." Also, use the Dealing with Feeling® communication game often. It gets beneath the facade and helps bring people out of denial.

9. **How can members be encouraged to attend regularly?**

Calling members or writing them a note will encourage them to be at the meeting. (Contacts are made by a person of the same sex.)

One of the benefits of an ongoing support group is that it's there when people are ready. Because people are at different stages in recovery, the number attending group will vary.

256 *Meeting How To*

> "For where two or three are gathered together in my name, I am there in the midst of them."
> Matthew 18:20 NKJV

10. **What should we do when only one or two show up for meeting?**

Commitment means holding the meeting regardless of how few show up. As a few begin to experience recovery, they will bring others to the meeting.

Remember to set up some extra chairs and ask God to fill them. See page 254, #5 for how to get the word out about your group.

11. **How can we get everyone to participate in the group discussion?**

- Approach your group with a warm, caring attitude. (Your nonverbal speaks louder than words.)
- Address people by their names so they will know they matter to you.
- Keep eye contact with all members. Even if someone says very little, a smile will make them feel included in the discussion.
- Let visitors know that sharing is voluntary. Sometimes newcomers sit through a meeting without comment, and that's okay.
- Ask people to be brief to allow time for others.
- Be open about your own struggles and lead by example.
- Treat people with respect rather than talk down to them.
- Draw out those who are quiet with open-ended questions such as, "What do you think about this?" or "How do you feel about that?"
- Glance around the room often to check facial expressions and body language. You may want to call on people who appear bored.
- Use the Dealing with Feeling® communication game to stimulate in-depth sharing.
- Thank those who share, especially when they are open about something that was difficult for them to discuss.

DON'T:

- Be a "know-it-all."
- Do most of the talking.
- Be afraid of brief silences.
- Tell others what to do.

> Honest feedback can help people recognize and admit their feelings.

12. **How can we help our group do a better job of listening to one another?**

Remind your group that active listening involves:

- Hearing what the person is not saying as well as what (s)he is saying.
- Restating what you hear the person saying.
- Accepting the person's feelings without trying to fix them.
- Thanking the person for sharing.

"Body language" (such as facial expression and tone of voice) reveals the person's true feelings. If the words and the nonverbal disagree, believe the nonverbal and reflect that back. For example, "I sense that you are angry," or "You seem to be hurting." Honest feedback can help people recognize and admit their feelings.

Meeting How To 257

> People take your example more seriously than your advice.
> John Baker

13. **What is cross-talk?**

Cross-talk is conversation during a meeting directed to an individual rather than the group. However, restating what has been said or sharing what has worked for us can be helpful. The key is to include all members in the discussion and avoid giving advice.

14. **Is sharing what works for us the same as giving advice?**

Not really. Giving advice is telling the other person what to do. Sharing what works for us focuses on personal experience. For example, you might say, "I've felt that way too. What helps me is..." If it's not overdone, people tend to be receptive to this approach.

Keep in mind that sponsor-mentors* may advise if it's done outside of group time. **"Where no counsel is, the people fall; but in the multitude of counselors, there is safety."** (Proverbs 11:14)
*See the definition of sponsor-mentor on page 203.

15. **How can we discourage long explanations and "pity parties?"**

Help prevent this problem by reading the Rule of Three (inside back cover) and the Guideline on SHARING (page 244) at the beginning of the share time.

However, people will occasionally get bogged down in the details of their problems. To move the discussion on, gently interrupt the story and say, "What I hear you saying is... Now, what do you think is a healthy way to handle this problem?" If appropriate, ask members to share how they have solved similar situations.

16. **What can we do to avoid having Dealing with Feeling® take the whole meeting?**

The Dealing with Feeling® communication game meets a vital need in the recovery process. But here's how to keep the game from taking the whole meeting. (However, an occasional meeting devoted entirely to open sharing or Dealing with Feeling® can provide a refreshing change.)

> Feelings need to be admitted, experienced, and released to God.

- Divide into subgroups of five or six.
- Keep within the approximate time limits in the rules of the game.
- Allow about half of the main part of the meeting for the game. If you see that time is going to run out, you can eliminate the feedback from other members. That way everyone can play at least one card.
- To use the game in a large group, choose one or two cards for group discussion.

17. **In addition to Dealing with Feeling,® how can we encourage open sharing in our group?**

Ask members open-ended questions such as "What victories or defeats did you experience this week?" Or ask them to share beginning with

258 *Meeting How To*

either of the following: "I let my problems overcome me when..." or "I overcame my problems when...".

18. How can "Go For The Goals" be used as a leader's guide?

We suggest following the "Way To Go" format on the inside back cover. After open sharing or Dealing with Feeling®, ask a member to read aloud one section of a Goal from "Go For The Goals" (Section Three). Next, ask someone to read the questions one at a time for discussion. Your group will readily respond to these thought-provoking questions.

Occasionally, a question will be answered before it is asked. Simply go on to the next one. However, don't be concerned about covering a certain amount of material at one meeting. Meaningful discussion is far more important.

If the conversation wanders, tactfully bring it back to the subject at hand. Keep the focus on how to apply the Goals to daily life. But keep the meetings flexible enough to encourage sharing.

19. How can we make it easier to listen to people's emotional pain?

After years of denial, people need a safe place to express and experience their pain. Remind the group that part of recovery is learning to feel and allowing others to do the same. Members will be more comfortable if they realize they are not responsible to remove each others' pain. Their role is to listen *prayerfully* and affirm the person for sharing.

20. What can be done if someone's emotions get out of control?

Support group provides a safe place to release emotions as long as the well-being of the group is not threatened. (Refer to Group Guideline #8 (UNITY) on page 245.)

If someone cries uncontrollably, try to distract him or her from emotional issues. Hand the person a Kleenex, and gently assure him or her that you're glad (s)he came to group. If you are unable to move the discussion on, tactfully suggest that someone accompany the person out of the room just long enough for him or her to calm down.

To deal with uncontrolled anger, reflect back what you think the person is saying and feeling. (Telling someone who's in a rage to calm down can make matters worse because you don't seem to understand the problem.) If the outburst continues, ask the person to step out for a few minutes to regain composure. In severe cases, do not allow the offender to attend group. Instead, refer him or her to a counselor or other appropriate help.

Fortunately, major disturbances rarely occur. When they do, handle the situation prayerfully, and follow the guidance of your sponsoring ministry.

> Do not be concerned about covering a certain amount of material at one meeting. Meaningful discussion is far more important.

> A good way to forget your troubles is to help others out of theirs.

Meeting How To 259

20. **What can we do to help members feel safe to share highly sensitive issues?**

Some groups close their meeting to outsiders. Closed membership may be particularly helpful for sex and love addictions, incest survivors, etc. (People wishing to join a closed group are screened by the servant-leaders and/or sponsoring ministry.)

Also, members can reserve highly sensitive issues for discussion with a sponsor or counselor. Group participation will increase the effectiveness of the one-on-one counseling.

21. **How can we help those who, because of a father's abuse, cannot relate to the concept of a loving heavenly Father?**

People who've been abused by their earthly father will identify first with Jesus as their friend. With that foundation, they will gradually come to relate to God as Father. **"No one comes to the Father except through me"** (John 14:6) is doubly true for abuse victims.

22. **How can we politely keep a person from rambling or commenting about every question?**

Before anyone shares, call attention to the Rule of Three on the inside back cover. Ask members to remind one another when the rule is being ignored. Also, read the Guideline, SHARING, (page 244, #7) with your group. If these measures fail, speak privately to the person after the meeting.

23. **How can we develop a fruitful prayer time for the group?**

- Open every meeting with a brief prayer. Also, hold a short prayer time at the end before closing in the Overcomer's Prayer.
- Use the prayer request note pad at every meeting. (Members' prayer requests may not be shared with outsiders.) Also, give opportunity to briefly share answers to prayer.
- Hold a group discussion on "Power Through Prayer" (page 205).
- Read the Guideline on PRAYER (page 245, #9) together.
- Study Goal Eight, DEVOTIONS, sections D and E (pages 159-161.)

24. **Is it okay to use handout sheets and other outside material at our meetings?**

We suggest that you make your Handbook and Dealing With Feeling® the main focus of the meeting. However, additional literature (such as the resources listed on page 210-212) can be helpful. You may want to get your sponsoring ministry's approval on supplemental material.

25. **What can we do for occasional variety in the suggested format?**

There's more than a year of weekly meetings in "Go For The Goals" without ever using the same material twice! However, nearly the entire Handbook is suitable for discussion. For example:

Prayers can't be answered unless they are prayed.

There's more than a year of weekly meetings in the "Going For The Goals" without ever using the same material twice!

> When we work, we work; when we pray, God works.

- Spend several meetings on "The Starting Line" (pages 15-39).
- Ask members to share what any of the illustrations at the beginning of each Goal (or elsewhere) mean to them.
- Read and discuss "What Is Christ-centered Recovery?" (page 9).
- Discuss the "Group Guidelines" (pages 244-245).
- Ask members to do "Who Needs Recovery?" on pages 10-11. Then discuss, "Where Are You?" (page 12).
- Discuss one of the interviews on pages 217-242 that you feel your group would identify with. Ask them to tell how they relate.
- Other excellent discussion material: The "Overcomer's Covenant" (page 199), "Meanings That Matter" (pages 202-203), "Power Through Prayer" (page 205), and "Avoiding Relapse" (page 209).

Topic discussions can be effective as well. Choose any subject that meets the needs of your group. For example, if you sense anger and resentment, spend a meeting discussing the problem. You might relate the short form of each Overcomer's Goal to your topic.

Speaker's meetings also give variety. Choose speakers whose lives demonstrate the Overcomer's Goals (regardless of whether they are a group member). Keep in mind that those who promote "instant" recovery will not be helpful to your group.

Occasionally, your group will enjoy spending an entire meeting on the Dealing with Feeling® communication game.

26. When do you suggest dividing into additional groups?

> If a group of twelve was adequate for Jesus, we would do well to follow His example.

When more than twelve members regularly attend a group, it becomes difficult for everyone to share. Dividing into subgroups helps a group multiply, providing each new group has qualified servant-leaders. (If a group of twelve was adequate for Jesus, we would do well to follow His example.)

With your sponsoring ministry, consider forming smaller groups dealing with specific life controlling problems. You may wish to hold a larger meeting for testimonies and united prayer before dividing into smaller discussion groups.

27. What is the special closing for Overcomers in Christ meetings?

Most of our groups use the Overcomer's Prayer found on the last page of the Handbook. Form a circle, join hands, and repeat the prayer together. While still holding hands, enthusiastically repeat the closing, "To overcome, keep coming over!"

Meeting How To 261

FREQUENTLY ASKED QUESTIONS

1. Why are the Overcomer's Goals not called steps?

By using Goals instead of steps, people will be less likely to confuse us with traditional twelve-step programs. The only time we say steps instead of Goals is when dealing with the penal system.

2. What obligation does the group have to report illegal activity?

The laws vary from place to place, so call your local authorities for information.

3. How can we deal with someone who breaks confidentiality?

Breaking confidentiality is a sure way to destroy a group. Therefore, read the Confidentiality Reminder (page 8) early in every meeting.

If a problem does occur, follow these biblical principles: talk to the offender and kindly, but firmly, let him or her know that confidentiality must be respected. If the problem continues, several mature members should meet with the offender. Warn that unless confidentiality is respected, (s)he will be unwelcome at future meetings.

4. Do you recommend that people be permitted to attend group under the influence of drugs or alcohol?

We wouldn't say that God won't work with those who are under the influence. However, disruptive behavior is unacceptable. See the Group Guideline, UNITY, on page 245. Anyone who persists in loud, boisterous behavior must be asked to leave. Keep the way open for the person to return if (s)he is willing to behave. It's up to you and your sponsoring ministry to prayerfully decide how to handle each case.

5. What is the Overcomers in Christ perspective on smoking as it relates to recovery?

Goal Three, HEALTH, deals with nicotine addiction and other health issues. While smoking is one of the more visible and deadly addictions, a fault-finding attitude is equally offensive to God. So pray for those who struggle with nicotine addiction, and let them recover at their own pace. (But keep your meetings smoke free to give people a breath of fresh air in more ways than one!)

> Gossip is discussing a problem with someone who is not part of the problem or part of the solution.

> How is it that we classify some sins as respectable when all sins are equally offensive to God?

262 *Frequently Asked Questions*

> God has no problems— only plans.
> Corrie ten Boom

6. **How can we handle the problem of members having different editions of the Handbook?**

We want groups to benefit from the best we can offer. Therefore, we encourage all servant-leaders to use the latest edition of the Handbook. Also, a few group copies would be helpful for use during meetings. Those who have the previous edition can use it to work on the Goals outside of group.

7. **What can we do about members who cannot afford a Handbook?**

With few exceptions, little can be gained by giving books away. Money that was previously used to feed addiction and dysfunction can be used to support recovery. (Inmates and institutional groups with no income receive their supplies from their sponsoring ministry or others.)

Some missions encourage residents to donate half of the funds toward their Handbook. Also, sponsoring ministries for institutional groups and programs can contact Overcomers in Christ about a license to photocopy the first six "Go For The Goals" lessons. (It is illegal to photocopy without written permission.)

8. **What is a sponsor-mentor?**

A sponsor-mentor is someone with at least two years in recovery who works one-on-one with another person of the same sex. The sponsor-mentor provides encouragement, accountability, and fellowship but does not assume responsibility for the sponsoree's progress. (Contact Overcomers in Christ for a sample Sponsor-Mentor Agreement.)

9. **What can we do about the shortage of sponsor-mentors?**

If all those who find recovery through Christ would reach out to others, more sponsor-mentors would be available. That's why we encourage those who overcome to continue in the group.

Groups usually have two servant-leaders experienced in recovery. Hopefully, they can each sponsor at least one person. Members without a sponsor can choose a partner of the same sex with whom to work on the Goals. Even people who are in early recovery can help one another if they're serious about spiritual growth.

> "If any of you lacks wisdom, ask God, who gives generously to all without finding fault, and it will be given."
> James 1:5

10. **Should a group leader meet one-on-one with a person who says a group setting makes him or her uncomfortable?**

Those who need one-on-one counseling can be referred to a counselor. However, if the person is of the same sex, there may be no problem meeting with him or her once in a public place. But we caution against devoting time to someone unwilling to get involved in the group. Instead, encourage him or her to get out of the comfort zone. (For one thing, manipulation will be less likely to occur.) After (s)he joins the group, someone could sponsor the person and give some individual attention.

Frequently Asked Questions 263

> "Everything should be done in a fitting and orderly way."
> 1 Corinthians 14:40

11. **Is it okay to invite people to group who don't know the Lord?**

Absolutely. The material on pages 15-39 can show anyone who is open how to become God's child. Also, the Overcomer's Goals lead people from wherever they are to victory in Christ. For example, a school teacher who proofed the third edition of our Handbook got saved in the process! It thrills us to see how the Lord uses the ministry to help people come to know Him in a personal way!

12. **Which recovery anniversaries usually get recognized and how?**

While the credit for victory goes to the Lord, it's important to enjoy recovery milestones together. The anniversaries that are usually celebrated are: one month, three months, six months, nine months, one year, one and a half years, two years, and every year thereafter.

O.I.C. Medallions and/or certificates (listed on our order form) are awarded by the sponsor-mentor or other servant-leader. Give the person being honored the opportunity to share a brief testimony.

13. **How can group members be encouraged to give?**

Giving benefits both the giver and the receiver. Here's how you can encourage your group members to share their resources:

- Take an offering at every meeting. Encourage all who can to give a dollar or more. Set an example by putting in at least a dollar yourself.
- Explain that offerings are used to meet group expenses and to support the Overcomers in Christ ministry.
- Occasionally discuss the Guideline, OFFERINGS, on page 245.
- Those who have no income can give by praying for the ministry and sending a short letter to us about how Overcomers has helped them.

> We make a living by what we get, but we make a life by what we give.

14. **How should group offerings be used?**

Group funds are used for group expenses such as babysitting or brochures if not provided by the sponsoring ministry. Also, love offerings can be sent to Overcomers in Christ to help us provide quality materials and service.

NOTE: Meeting the needs of members should be an individual choice rather than using group funds. Otherwise, group unity can be threatened.

15. **What should we do if a member becomes suicidal?**

Take any threat of suicide seriously. If possible, remove the intended means of suicide. Respond with love rather than shock or judgment. Call 911 or another crisis intervention number, and stay with the person until help arrives.

16. **How can we help the person who sincerely wants to move forward but seems to be stuck?**

First, if there is any doubt whatever that the person is born again, go over "How To Become God's Child" (Section Two) with him or her.

Second, consider leading the person through the Steps to Freedom (Section Four). Many people who were previously immobilized have found freedom in Christ in this manner. Third, make sure the person has an effective support team (including a sponsor-mentor). Finally, see #17 below.

17. How do we know when to refer to a professional?

When a situation is too difficult for the group to cope with, the person should be referred to a pastor, counselor, physician or crisis intervention specialist. Also, make referrals whenever people are dangerous to themselves or others.

18. What can we do if we suspect that a person is under demonic influence?

Deliverance work is not for the inexperienced. Try to locate a pastor or Christian counselor who is knowledgeable about deliverance and can lead the person through the "Steps To Freedom" on pages 45-96. Also, we recommend that all servant-leaders educate themselves by reading at least one book on the occult from the "Recommended Resources" on pages 210-212.

19. How long should it take a person to work through "Go For The Goals"?

> *The key is to absorb and apply the lessons rather than rush through them.*

The key is to absorb and apply the lessons rather than rush through them. By doing one section of a Goal every weekday, "Go For The Goals" can be completed in three months. (A group would need to meet five times a week to move at that pace.)

20. What do you think about having members write in the workbook during group?

The workbook is to be completed *outside* of group time. Otherwise, the meeting becomes a class rather than a support group. Member interaction and sharing would be greatly hindered. (In the institutional setting, a class could supplement the support group meetings but not replace them.)

21. Do you recommend inviting group members into our homes?

It's not usually advisable to invite the group as a whole into your home. There are too many unknown factors. It is wise to wait until you know an individual well before you decide whether to invite him or her into your home.

22. We hear a lot about accountability and a lot about boundaries. How do the two relate?

Healthy relationships involve a balance between the two:

Accountability *without* boundaries = bondage and codependence
Boundaries *without* accountability = isolation and independence
Accountability *with* boundaries = healthy interdependence

Frequently Asked Questions 265

INSTITUTIONAL GROUPS

1. **What tools do you offer to evaluate people's need for recovery?**

   "Who Needs Recovery?" on pages 10-11 will help you evaluate people's needs. However, the testimonies we receive tell us that anyone can benefit from working the "Go For The Goals" lessons and attending support group.

2. **How many meetings should disciples be required to attend?**

   We recommend at least three to five mandatory meetings each week for newcomers. One meeting a week will not be enough to overcome deeply ingrained habits.

   After three months of recovery and abstinence, your disciples could be required to attend fewer meetings. (Perhaps two each week.) However, if they return to their sin addiction, people should be required to attend three to five meetings weekly until they again have at least three months of recovery. If compulsive behavior continues, the person should be referred to treatment or other help and dismissed. This plan will help eliminate people who aren't serious and improve morale for both residents and staff.

   Disciples should be encouraged to supplement in-house meetings with outside ones. Such interaction builds a bridge with a positive peer group. We suggest providing transportation and a reliable person to accompany disciples to outside meetings. (Check our directory to locate an existing group. Or show a Recovery Kit to the leaders of a Bible-believing church that has shown interest in working with your disciples, and ask them to consider starting a group.)

3. **How can we motivate disciples to attend group?**

   People may try to avoid any meeting that causes them to face their problems. But one way to encourage cooperation is to allow them to substitute support group for other studies or meetings. Discipleship will be most effective by meeting people at their point of need.

4. **How can we economically provide recovery material for our rapidly changing clientele?**

   If your group has a high turnover, contact Overcomers in Christ for a license to photocopy the first six "Go For The Goals" lessons. However, as soon as their commitment to recovery is definite, each person needs a complete Handbook.

5. **With the constant turnover in our group, how can we provide continuity in the lessons?**

   People can benefit from a support group regardless of which Goal the group might be discussing. Continuity comes from working the

> One meeting a week will not be enough for people with deeply ingrained habits.

> No one who works for the Lord can afford to despise a single soul. Any contempt expressed in attitude or deed disqualifies a person as a servant of God.
> Watchman Nee

266 *Institutional Groups Only*

> *When it's all said and done, there's more said than done.*

lessons consecutively with a sponsor-mentor or partner.

We encourage you to require your disciples to write out the answers to the "Go For The Goals" lessons. They'll study the Goals more thoroughly and internalize them better. Keep in mind that the workbook is to be completed outside of group time. (If someone cannot read or write, a partner can work with him or her.)

6. **We have difficulty finding qualified group leaders. What do you suggest?**

Ministries with the most effective groups integrate O.I.C. into their overall program (rather than treating it as an extra). Those who are responsible for discipling and/or counseling take ownership and responsibility for the group. If qualified volunteer leaders can be found, that's great. But if not, the program moves forward with staff leadership. Everyone wins as the disciples experience healing and the ministry fulfills its mission.

7. **What can we do to help our disciples avoid relapse and continue to progress after they leave us?**

They need to be integrated into a healthy body of believers. However, those who've been institutionalized experience cultural clash with the church. They don't relate to the church, and the church doesn't relate to them. Your disciples will more likely succeed with an O.I.C. support group in the institution *and* in their eventual church home. Remember, people gravitate toward the familiar. The chart below illustrates how O.I.C. can ease hurting people into church.

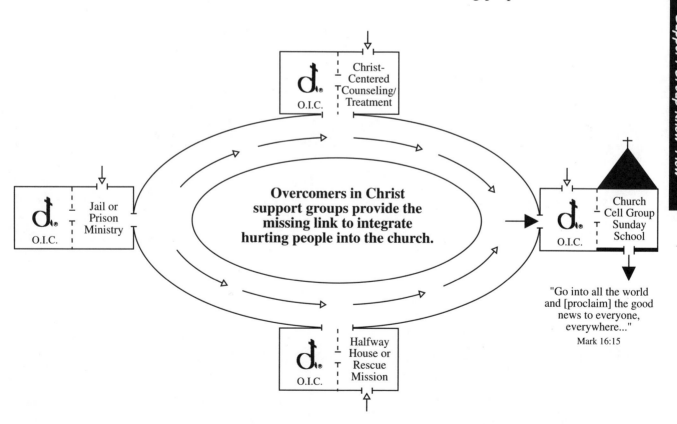

Institutional Groups Only 267

Live each day
in the light of
the Lord's
soon return.

Jesus said:

"Behold I am coming soon!
My reward is with me,
and I will give to everyone
according to what he has done.
Yes, I am coming soon!"

Amen.
Come Lord Jesus.

Revelation 22:12, 20

Phone Numbers

For mutual support, remember to contact other members (of the same sex) between meetings. Also, we encourage you to choose a sponsor-mentor whom you can call often for prayer, support, and fellowship. (See the definition of a sponsor-mentor on page 203.)

Don't wait for others to reach out to you. To find a friend, be one!

Remember the banana? Every time it leaves the bunch it gets skinned.

Name	Phone

Notes

Give people
a piece of your
heart not a piece
of your mind.
John Baker

Notes

Description of an overcomer:

A mind through which Christ thinks, a heart through which Christ loves, a voice through which Christ speaks, a hand through which Christ helps.

The Overcomer's Prayer

Lord, help us to overcome our fears, loneliness, guilt, and self-will through your Son, Jesus Christ.

Give us strength to obey your loving command: "Do not be overcome by evil, but overcome evil with good."*

In Jesus' name, Amen

*Romans 12:21

If your troubles are deep-seated or long standing, try kneeling!